MW00576241

CRYSTAL CORRIDOR OF LIGHT

THE STARSEED HIGHWAY

BETHEL BARR

Design and distribution by Bublish, Inc.

ISBN: 978-1-647045-77-7 (eBook)
ISBN: 978-1-647045-42-5 (paperback)

Contents

$\mathcal{D}$edication

The writing of this book has come from my heart. My search for the "right" words to use as a dedication kept coming back to this message from Archangel Ariel. There are no words of mine to express a dedication that would be as profound and full of truth as these words from the Goddess, so I am passing her loving words on to you, reader.

Many years ago, I purchased a book containing channeled information from this archangel. The book inspired me in numerous ways, and the truth that issued forth resonated with me and fascinated me. I had never read a book like this one, and I have been an avid reader of various authors since childhood.

I still own and treasure this wonderful work of literature that was so lovingly given to humanity. I especially love the words of dedication uttered by Archangel Ariel.

ARCHANGEL ARIEL—
THE MOTHER GODDESS

We wish to dedicate this work to
all of those souls
who have dared to look,
who have risked finding,
and who have faced tremendous fear
in what they have found.

Those souls who have followed their hearts
and have discovered
what their journey has led them to find.
And having found, have shared.
And having shared,
have continued.

~ Archangel Ariel

The book is *Interview with an Angel* by Stevan J. Thayer and Linda Sue Nathanson, PhD. (Published in the United States and Canada, May 1999, by Dell Publishing.)

$\mathcal{P}$reface

The Starseed Highway is a most remarkable road—a road of adventure!—and contained within that one great adventure are numerous other adventures and experiences.

Since Creation is about balance, there are often situations that offset the excitement and joy of "being." Those situations can be extremely challenging, sapping our strength and stretching our determination and dedication to the limit.

Each moment can be filled with joy or sorrow, comfort or pain, sunshine or clouds, ease or difficulty. It is whatever we choose using our God-given gift of free will, and each situation we encounter along the way, whether we sail through or muddle through, adds to our Soul growth. It is an extraordinary journey, even though we suffer now and then; through that suffering, we learn and grow.

I have always been a Seeker, even in my younger years when I didn't realize what the word meant. My passion to learn about the Great Unknown was what lured me ever onward. After many years of searching, I realized that great desire, the urge to go forward, was the gentle prodding of my Higher Self.

This book is a synopsis of my learning to this date. I will never stop learning. To do so would be to stop evolving, and evolution is never ending.

My writing is designed to assist others on the spiritual path using my own life experiences; it is to help all those souls who are interested in moving forward in evolution through learning about the Great Unknown, the Ancient Wisdom, and the world of Spirit.

It is to demonstrate the numerous ways to advance in consciousness through utilizing the various tools we are gifted with.

It is to aid in illuminating the darkness of confusion, fear, doubt, negativity, sorrow, and anxiety by reaching for Spirit through the heart space, using Love as the answer to everything.

I would like to pass on to the reader a quotation I received from my Higher Self. It is a profound quotation that I have found very helpful as I travel my journey of discovery.

Embrace your challenges
Forgive your stumbles
Celebrate your victories.

~ Bethel

$\mathcal{I}$ntroduction

THE HUMAN ME

Words have always been important to me, beginning in my school years. Writing an essay was far more interesting and rewarding than trying to solve a math problem.

I love the way words can be put together to make sense of something, they are magical and powerful. The "power of the pen" should never, ever be discounted. Short stories, blogs, and essays are easy to write—but a book? That is a very different endeavor.

I never consciously aspired to write a book. However, one bright and beautiful day, I realized that writing a book, this book, was part of my life plan. And so, here I am.

The path to enlightenment has taken me through many years and countless experiences, and those wonderful, rich experiences are contained within this book to assist other Seekers on their path of adventure. The love and commitment I feel for this planet and humanity is deep and enduring, which is why I am putting these words together now. I am in service to the Mother, to those souls who are struggling with their own journey, to humanity and beyond.

When I first learned that writing was a huge part of my mission, I was stunned. What did I know about writing a book? I was advised to "come from the heart." So I did, so I am, and so I will continue to do so.

I was born near the end of WWII and spent my childhood and teenage years in a remote area of the province of Saskatchewan, Canada. Our family was not rich in money, but we had much more than material things. We had safety, security, and love from parents and siblings. Healthy, wholesome food was plentiful, and we relished the simplicity of life in those long-ago days.

During childhood, we were gifted with the wonderful phenomena of nature, partly due to the abundance of natural beauty surrounding us. It was not unusual to witness the splendor of the aurora borealis as the blue, green and crimson lights danced across the indigo sky. There were times when Dad would call us to come and watch from a safe vantage point as storm clouds billowed and swirled in the distance. Perhaps he would show us a particular spring waterfall or bird's nest that we were told not to interfere with. Nature was a learning paradise and ever present.

We grew up listening to the whisper of the wind as it blew through the top branches of the mighty pine trees that were so plentiful in our area. We huddled down in bed, pulled our blankets closer around us, and listened to the eerie howl of the timber wolf as it called to its mate on a moonlit night.

Running barefoot in the yard in summer, maybe chasing the chickens when Mom wasn't looking, creating our own fun, and being inventive with toys, since store-bought ones were nonexistent, were all part of daily life. The great outdoors was our playground, and running unfettered, free, innocent, and feeling at one with nature was our life.

When autumn arrived, we enjoyed the abundance of the vegetable garden, the exciting times of grain harvesting, and the generous Thanksgiving meals and family gatherings.

Winters were harsh in that area of the world, so we settled indoors, enjoyed the warmth of a woodstove and heater, and made our own entertainment by playing card games as a family and listening to my father play his violin. Occasionally while he played, my mother would teach us the rudiments of old-time dance steps.

We made good use of what we had to play with during the winter—snow and lots of it. Snow tunnels, sledding, ice-skating, and more family gatherings.

Springtime brought new growth, new challenges, and more work. Life was simple but not very easy, and the demands were often strenuous and involved a lot of hard work for everyone, for it meant our very survival. We learned that if we wanted to eat, we had to work, from weeding the large garden to walking for hours in search of a few wild berries for Mom to preserve in jars for the next winter.

My life learning began early. I learned that when times are challenging, it is best to work together as a family toward the greater good of all. Although humble, life was rich in what truly mattered: love, safety, and good health.

One day while outdoors playing in the woods, I saw something flitting from tree to tree. It presented itself as a dense shadow, dark gray, adult-sized, but indistinct. I watched it curiously, wondering what it was that I was seeing. *I'll ask Mom*, I thought. *Mom knows everything.*

Well, my mom was a very busy farm lady, too busy to listen to the prattle of what she assumed was a child's imagination, and she told me to run and play. I did what she said, but I never forgot what I saw that lovely, sunny, summer day so long ago.

Many years later, I learned that dense shadow was my very own guardian angel, and the experience of the moment was planned preincarnate. I also learned that Spirit has countless ways to get our attention and communicate with us.

Curiosity has always been with me. During childhood, some of the questions that plagued me were:

- How far is up?
- What is up there in the sky?
- What is the sky? Why is it blue?
- How does an airplane stay in the sky?

The questions changed as I grew older:

- What is infinity?
- What do I need to do to understand it?
- Where shall I look for answers?
- Who will tell me?

The big one for me was:

- Who is God?
- What is God?
- Why is God male?
- What is a soul?
- How did we get here?
- Who am I?
- Where did I come from?
- Why am I here?

Naive as I was, I thought teachers, pastors, or priests should know the answers, but of course they did not. My questions only irritated them.

My avid curiosity never waned, but I did move on in life, neared adulthood, moved away from my parents' home, and established myself in the banking industry in a nearby town.

I became familiar with the term "gender equality," or rather "gender inequality," and the patriarchal system that was prevalent at the time. All those important events in my life only brought more questions:

- Why did men earn more money than women for doing the same work?
- Where were all the female managers?
- Why were men offered the most favorable opportunities?

Once again, life did not make sense.

During the early 1960s, I met and married my life mate. A few years later, we moved to a small town in central Saskatchewan, and that is where my paranormal experiences began.

Déjà vu was the first of those experiences to show itself. I would be doing a normal, mundane household chore, perhaps making a pudding for my small children, and then, for a nanosecond, I just *knew* I had already experienced the same situation!

Next to appear was precognition. Of course, I did not know the name of it. I only knew it was very puzzling. I *knew* the phone would ring before it did. I *knew* that my good friend would knock on my door and come in for coffee. One of my young sons had an "imaginary" friend he would converse with, even holding the door open to allow the friend to enter the house. They were strange occurrences that caused more unanswered questions.

Ever curious, I experimented with a Ouija board. I am unable to remember where it came from or why it was in my possession, but I was fascinated with it. I could make it move without physically touching it, and that frightened me, so I got rid of it and have never wanted another one. It was all just more and more puzzles to mull over.

In desperation, I finally turned to religion, and after making a few attempts to read the Bible cover to cover, I gave it up. Somehow, I knew my answers did not lie within those pages. Something very important was missing from my life, but I didn't know what it was.

Eventually, both my husband and I left the banking system, opened a small business, and raised our three sons. The metaphysical world lay dormant in my life for a time.

Then, in the mid-1980s, my parents became ill—both with degenerative, terminal diseases. My father suffered from Alzheimer's, and my beautiful mother from amyotrophic lateral sclerosis (commonly known as ALS or Lou Gehrig's disease). They both transitioned to "the other side" in the spring and summer of 1990—my mother in April, and my father in August.

Having to witness both of my beloved parents suffer through these two horrific diseases propelled me firmly and fully onto my path as a spiritual Seeker, and I have never looked back.

Throughout the years of 1987 to 1990, I avidly searched for any information I could find about life, death, God, the afterlife, near-death experiences—anything that would bring answers to ease the pain of watching two people I loved so much suffer. My father's disease caused him to not recognize me, so I was unable to communicate with him, but my mother was mentally alert to the end of her earthly life.

We often spoke about what would or could happen to her soul after the death of her physical body, and she was open to any information I could provide. She was very interested in learning about the afterlife and was comfortable discussing that sensitive topic, so chatting with her about her illness was not difficult. During these conversations, I asked her to contact me after she passed if she was willing and able to do so. She agreed to grant my request.

About a month after my mother passed over to the other side, I was told by a good friend that a psychic was in the area and was asked if I wanted to go to see her. Of course I said a resounding, "Yes!" It was an amazing experience, and what a special gift she gave to me!

As soon as I sat in front of her, I began to weep and told her my mother had only died a month prior. She smiled and said, "I know; she is here with us." On that day so long ago, my earth mother gave me a personal message that only she and I would understand. She did indeed contact me!

My earth father transitioned about four months later, and since that summer of 1990, I have received visitations and messages from both of my earth parents. During one of the visitations, my mother gave me a big hug. She walked toward me with her arms open wide and hugged me. I saw her face, I saw her long, dark hair and her smile. I felt the hug; it was real. The event did not happen in the physical world, it happened in what is referred to as "the astral plane" or "the spirit world."

When my father stopped by one night, I saw him in a group of people, and his face was very clear. I saw his snowy white hair, his brilliant blue eyes, and his big smile. He took my hand, and we began to dance. As we twirled around the room, I asked my father, "Can you tell me what it is like where you are?" His smile faded. He said, "No," and then he was gone. I thought if he ever came back, I would not ask any questions of him!

During my teen years, we often went to a dance in the local town, and when my father danced with me, I was so proud and happy! I loved to dance with him, I thought he was the most handsome dad in the room, and I felt like a princess as we danced around the big hall.

When we are visited by loved ones who have transitioned, they will most often present themselves in a way we find most familiar. Being able to dance with my dad was a very important event in my life, so that is how he presented himself to me.

This part of my writing has a specific purpose, and that is to allow other Seekers to know that there is life after death of the physical body and there are times when our loved ones do contact us if we are willing to receive their messages and presence without fear and if we trust in Spirit. It is also to demonstrate how my own journey flowed and that each step contributed to and enriched my evolutionary process.

THE JOURNEY CONTINUES

Each soul's journey is unique and special. I chose preincarnate to be what I like to think of as a "late bloomer," meaning I was older than many other Seekers when I fully embraced the spiritual path. My first contract was with my children, and when that contract was complete, I was able to move on and concentrate more on my spirituality. And I did that with gusto!

As soon as my three sons were adults and on their own, the paranormal experiences became more frequent, and I realized that the journey of a dedicated and conscious Starseed can be, and often is, a very lonely and confusing time, and so it was for me. I desperately wanted to meet with and talk to other people like myself, people I could relate to who would understand what was happening to me and why.

The search was never ending. I began to look for classes in the area. I needed more information about the Great Unknown and left no stone unturned during my quest. The more I craved answers, the more I received, and that of course brought forth the desire to know more and more.

What was behind that next unopened door? What wonderful treasure lived there? What and where was the key that opened the door? Who could I ask?

The answers always came; my spiritual team of angels and guides never let me down. My task was to keep searching, and then the door would open. With each tentative or bold step came more treasures of knowledge! It was, and still is, delightful!

I now know nothing is coincidence, nothing happens by accident. The Universe does not make mistakes.

Everything is planned with precision. And that was the way it was, and still is, with my journey through this life.

Perhaps when in conversation with someone, a name would crop up, a new teacher I could learn from, and I always took advantage of the new opportunity.

THE NEW MILLENNIUM

In the early 2000s, my husband and I began to travel, and one of our trips took us to the state of Arizona. We both loved the energy of the Phoenix area and the desert, so we decided to spend our winter months there. In the fall of 2007, we became one of the many "snowbirds" to occupy the Valley of the Sun.

Now I had the best of both worlds—winters in Arizona and summers in Alberta. Our retirement flowed along smoothly. We enjoyed the many wonderful sights, sounds, and smells of the Sonoran Desert, which is sub-tropical and the most diverse and complex desert in North America.

The treasures in the area are many: exotic scenes to explore, wonderful hiking trails, golfing, beautiful mountains and valleys, an abundance of sunshine, and just enough rainfall to make the plants happy. There are outdoor areas to enjoy, and the region is known as a very spiritual area. I can attest to that.

There are numerous places to attend spiritual classes, yoga, and many other modalities that can and do entice the spiritual Seeker. Plus, the people in the valley are friendly, with open hearts. The Sonoran Desert is also the home of the famous saguaro cactus, which I think of as the sentinel of the desert.

One of my favorite activities is walking, a daily practice. On these walks, I experience peace, joy, and sometimes even adventures. It was during one of my early morning walks that a unique experience happened to me. Every morning when I walked under a particular streetlight on my way to a nearby grocery store for the morning newspaper, the streetlight would go out and then come back on.

At first, I thought it was an electrical glitch of some kind, but after seeing it happen morning after morning, I decided it must be Spirit communicating with me. Maybe it was angels or guides, I was not sure; I just knew it was not earthly. I was thrilled, but as with anything that I experienced, more questions arose. Who was it? What did they want? Why were they contacting me? No answer—at least, not then.

Time went on, and we moved back to Alberta for the summer months. The streetlight phenomenon continued there during my early morning walks. After a time, I began to take a pencil and a small scrap of paper with me, jot down the sequences of "blinks," hurry home, and decipher my scribbling.

It was fun, it was an adventure, it was exciting, and I loved it. The bonus was that I received messages from the angels through these "blinks," such as:

- Be at peace. The angels are all around you.
- Change is coming.
- Monitor your thoughts.

This experience pushed me further along the path to enlightenment, and soon I learned about the power of color therapy and sound therapy. Such a wonderful, amazing, magical, intriguing journey I was on! Occasionally, earth life would present itself, but mostly my time was spent learning, growing, and experimenting with all things spiritual. There was no stopping me.

THE STARRY ME

My spiritual journey was filled with many pleasurable experiences, and one of those was a yearly visit to a psychic, a channel who would connect with the higher dimensions and bring through messages for me. It was always a wonderful time. I would await the scheduled day with great anticipation and then eagerly listen to what the magical tarot cards had in store for me. It is impossible to relate in words what those experiences were like. They were nourishment for my soul.

During one of those visits, I explained my streetlight experiences, and the psychic told me that she knew of a powerful medium who had been channeling the archangels and angels for twenty-five years. One more door was opening for me, and this time, it was a huge door!

This lovely lady gave me the contact information for the channeler of angels, I made the contact, and my life changed.

As long as I live, I will never forget the first words that came from Spirit through that very gifted Channel of Light:

"Greetings. My name is Lucinda, and I am your guardian angel."

My guardian angel, through that beautiful channel, told me she was communicating with me through the streetlights blinking on and off, and she explained the difference between guardian angels and spirit guides. Spirit guides come and go throughout the life stream, but the guardian angel never, ever leaves; he or she is the one constant in the life of an incarnated soul.

It was a lot of information to take in, and my feelings were of indescribable joy and elation. It was so humbling to realize that this great Being would chat with me. How naive I was at that time! Later, I learned that all the angels and guides are just waiting for their disciple to want to communicate with them; we just need to hold the intention and then make the effort.

That was a major turning point in my spiritual life, and I was totally committed to learning more. It was as if a huge, brilliantly lit doorway had opened for me, and the desire to explore every inch, every nook and cranny, was front and center in my life.

Books regarding the world of Spirit still captivated me as I delved into them and soaked up every word. I eventually found other like-minded people, and we would come together in groups to share our experiences, our trials, and our joys. I was no longer "different." I finally found my niche. I finally "fit" somewhere!

I continued my search for truth. Then, one day, I heard the name "Goddess Ishtar." I was at once enthralled and determined to explore this topic further. The next time I was able to converse with my newfound psychic and channeler of angels, I asked why the name Ishtar had caught my interest. This was the answer that came through from the Spirit world:

"Because you are a Star person."

I was completely shocked into silence. After a few moments, I asked in a small voice, "What is a Star person?"

The answer from Spirit, through the gifted psychic, was, "You are not from here. You are from another planet."

That day, I learned that the latest star system I'd inhabited was the Pleiades Star Constellation, and the planet I was most recently from was Erra.

All of this took place in 2007 to 2009. At that time, I knew there were extraterrestrials "out there" somewhere, but I had no idea I was one of them!

Since that time, I have realized that we are all eternal beings; we are from nowhere and everywhere. We just make stops along the way on numerous planets, in various galaxies and universes. I have a heart connection with many areas of space—Arcturus, Lyra, Jupiter, Venus, Orion, and so on—because I have spent incarnations and time throughout the cosmos. We all have. So, we are not specifically from any one planet, although we most often relate to the latest area of habitation.

More and more, I began to identify with the Starry part of myself, and even though I loved the feeling, it caused some degree of sadness and longing. The more I remembered my life in the stars, the more longing I experienced. It's called "having a foot in each world." It is often difficult to stay grounded on planet Earth when the heart wanders into the Heavenworlds.

As the knowledge continued to flow, more consciousness expansion occurred within my Self. I came to the understanding that I am on a mission, and that is my first task. In order to complete that task to my own satisfaction,

I need to stay grounded with boots firmly planted on this planet for now.

Next on my list was to learn to meditate. Meditating alone with the purpose of connecting with Spirit is different than sitting through a guided meditation, where all one needs to do is listen to the guidance of the leader and focus on those words. Meditating alone is more difficult, at least for me. I initially had trouble focusing my mind and clearing my thoughts.

My guardian angel said to place my errant thoughts in a bubble and set it aside. Meditation is all about visualization and intention, and I loved learning about it. She said the ego wants to keep control and not allow the disciple's conscious mind to take over. I eventually learned not to worry about my random thoughts, to let them drift by and continue with my meditative quest.

I became a determined and dedicated meditator, and through that process, I developed a strong connection and bond with my Higher Self and my team of angels in the higher dimensions.

My occasional sessions with the psychic, the channeler of the angels, ended in 2009, when she transitioned back Home. I missed her very much, but Spirit had other plans in mind for me.

WINTER OF 2011 AND 2012

The winter of 2011 ushered in the notable year of 2012, which was significant in the spiritual community because it was the onset of a magical year that would culminate in the end of the infamous Mayan calendar. The Mayan calendar ended with December 2012, and December 21—the winter solstice—was indeed a powerful day cosmically.

In numerology, 2012 is a "five." The number five means *change,* and change was about to transpire throughout the world and for me personally. We as a spiritual community were hoping for a grand collective awakening of humanity, something akin to the Harmonic Convergence of 1987, when thousands of people around the world came together in consciousness and meditated on creating peace worldwide. It worked! There was a huge awakening from that global meditation, and now, once again, maybe something amazing would happen in 2012! It did happen, as more and more souls woke up to the truth, and it is still happening to this day in 2022.

While in Arizona that winter of 2011 and 2012, I came upon a lovely New Age bookstore and decided to check it out. These bookstores have always intrigued me, for they are filled with wonderful, mysterious, magical, mystical things: incense, crystals, Buddha statues, books, and treasures of all kinds.

I had heard of a gifted metaphysician who worked in the New Age bookstore, and the day I visited, he was there working with a group of other psychics. I later learned that he also was a teacher of the Ancient Wisdom and hosted classes at that location. Curious to meet this individual, I decided to contact him for an appointment.

During the initial reading and session, he told me that I should teach. I was puzzled and a bit confused. I had no plans to teach anyone. I wanted to learn and have someone teach me!

However, those words stuck with me, and so I began to move forward on the advice, feeling my way along blindly. It wasn't that difficult, because as soon as I made the first effort in that direction, the doors once again began to open, and everything just flowed. That is the way Spirit works. Spirit will assist us, but only if we take the first step toward helping ourselves. They cannot do it all for us.

There was a small room at the far end of my house that did not have a door, so I bought a privacy screen, told a few acquaintances about my new venture, and then waited… It all worked out. I hosted this small meeting once a week for two to seven people. I began to receive short messages from Spirit, which I would write down and then tentatively disclose the information to my small group. It felt a bit daunting but also thrilling. I was hooked!

My seeking never stopped, and when I found something I thought would be of interest to my small group, I would pass it on to them in the next meeting. Short meditations would come to my attention, and soon I was taking the group through a guided meditation, which pleased us all. It was always so rewarding for me to see someone begin to open to Spirit and "see" or "feel" something delightful during those meditations.

The doors continued to open as I followed the steps before me. I learned the ancient practice of Reiki; more information came to me regarding tarot cards; I learned to respect the fascinating power of energy; and was intrigued by the world of crystals as I discovered the uniqueness of each gem.

Another interesting experience happened during that time. I learned about the beautiful and spiritual tones of crystal singing bowls. The first time I heard someone playing the bowls, the vibrations affected my soul deeply and profoundly. As with so many spiritual experiences, I find it a challenge to come up with the words to describe my feelings. The good thing was that lifelong questions were being answered and the world was beginning to make sense.

I learned the healing power of massage therapy, and so many opportunities for knowledge arose. I also practiced the ancient art of Tai Chi. It seemed as if this was what I had been missing and waiting for my whole life.

All of these wonderful, captivating, and enchanting experiences nourished my soul.

Through my spiritual connections, I heard about three women who hosted a group that did angel readings. One more golden opportunity was given to me to explore! I loved that group! We would sit as couples, one to choose the deck of tarot cards and one to be the reader.

It was my first attempt at publicly trying to bring through messages from Spirit, and at first, I would receive only a word or two—enough to pass on a message. But that expanded the more I worked at it, and soon I realized I loved bringing messages forth from Spirit! What a thrill it was!

It was at one of these angel card meetings that I was propelled onto the next step of my ladder.

As I was leaving the room, I gave one of the organizers a hug and thanked her. She said to me, "If you ever want to hold a workshop, we have room for you." I thanked her and walked to my car, thinking, *Where the dickens did that come from?*

I drove home with many thoughts bouncing around in my head. *Now what shall I do? I don't know anything about holding a workshop! How will I make that happen? Oh, woe is me.* Well, I needn't have worried, Spirit already had it all worked out, and the plan unfolded with perfection as I diligently followed the guidance provided.

As fate would have it, I needed eye surgery a day before the meeting was scheduled to happen, but nothing was going to stop me. Black eye and bandage, I was there. Approximately twenty souls showed up to hear me, and I was terrified! It all went well though. There is very little, if any, judgment at these meetings, and that is the general energy of a group of Seekers: they are so busy trying to learn and forge their way ahead that they do not have the time nor the inclination to judge others.

My teaching was progressing, and for a few months, I continued to hold classes under the umbrella of those three wonderful ladies, all the while gaining experience for the next step on my journey. In November 2012, I realized I was ready to start my own group with my own venue, and I did just that. But first, I needed a name for my group, and I had no idea what that would be.

We all have what are called the Four Clairs of Intuition:

- Clairaudience — clear hearing
- Clairsentience — clear feeling or clear sensing
- Clairvoyance — clear seeing
- Claircognizance — clear knowing

My psychic strength lies in my "knowingness," and coming in second is my clear sensing or clear feeling. I just "know" things, and I "sense" or "feel" things. I trust the knowing and the feeling, and that trust has been very beneficial to me on my spiritual path.

One day, I just knew what the name of my group would be: The Crystal Corridor of Light Edmonton Group began November 2012, and the Crystal Corridor of Light Gold Canyon/East Valley Group came into being November 2014.

At the beginning, I would host meetings in Alberta during the summer and in Arizona during the winter months; five months in Arizona and seven months in Alberta. It has been a huge learning experience. All the souls who have sat with me during those meetings over the years have enriched my life in a variety of ways that no other situations could match.

During a meeting with my group, a member asked if anyone wanted to join him in an experiment. He suggested that whoever was interested should meet him in Lightbody atop the Parliament building in our city at a specific time of the night. Meeting another soul in Lightbody simply means we hold the intention, then astral travel. Our physical bodies stay, and the soul or Lightbody can travel anywhere.

Ever curious, I decided to give it a try, and through the suggestion of that member, I was introduced to yet another exciting, interesting experience! When I went to bed that evening, I held the intention to astral travel to the specified location, and in the morning, I realized that I did indeed travel and remembered being there.

I remembered the semidarkness and wearing a long, flowing garment. I could not see the color. I was aware that we were on top of the building, very high up. As with all my new spiritual adventures, it was amazing!

While in Arizona, I sought venues where I could attend group classes. They are plentiful in the Valley, and I took advantage of as many as I was able to. A few of the classes offered information regarding UFOs, which at that time was a whole new area for me. I did my usual and soaked up the information!

As Seekers, our life paths are each different and yet similar in many ways. We all seek information about the unknown. Through the variety of opportunities in the Valley, I blossomed and grew in spiritual maturity.

I met Starseeds who had the ability to do remote viewing, meaning they were able to project their consciousness somewhere outside of the physical body and "see" what was happening in another area of the world. I later learned that this method was used during the great world wars, WWI and WWII, to spy on and gain knowledge of the enemy's plans and was used by both sides of the warring factions.

I was privileged to meet a talented teacher who took me through the exciting and fascinating world of shamanism, astrology, and numerology. I absorbed each moment of all these wonderful experiences and learned much. I found a teacher who assisted me in improving my channeling of the higher dimensions. It is nothing one can "learn," I realized; it is more about gaining the confidence to trust oneself. It can be a long or short road to reaching that level of self-confidence.

The Valley of the Sun in Arizona is rife with UFO sightings! During the spring of 1997, an "otherworldly" phenomenon occurred in the Valley, witnessed by hundreds of people and shown on the local television news.

According to Wikipedia, the Phoenix Lights were a series of widely sighted, unidentified flying objects— UFOs—observed in the skies over Arizona, Nevada, and the Mexican state of Sonora on March 13, 1997.

I did not witness those UFOs, but during my many years in the Valley, I have seen a few.

MORE DOORS TO OPEN

The autumn of 2015 found me on yet another new venture. I decided to begin writing blog posts. I had information, good information, and I was passing it on to others in my group, so the next step was to put it in writing.

I found someone to construct a web page for me, also called Crystal Corridor of Light (www.crystalcorridorlight.

com), and began to write blogs. I published my first blog November 28, 2015.

When a Starseed is consciously aware of who they are and where they are from, the guidance given by Spirit, the events, excitement, and experiences seem endless. There were times when I felt as if I was on a roller coaster and had to hang on or lose control. There was so much coming into my life in the way of information that would later become knowledge. I soaked it up and asked for more! And it came.

My searching led me to a Lightworker, an amazing, gifted woman by the name of Judy Satori, and through her I discovered the Language of the Stars—the Light Language. I came upon her website many years ago, was fascinated by her unique gifts, and decided to order a CD titled *The Song of Lyra*. The music is hauntingly beautiful, and interspersed within the music is Light Language spoken by Judy Satori. The music and Light Language I heard that day awoke something primal and ancient within me.

I felt a close connection with Lyra, a familiarity I did not fully understand. It brought an emotion to the surface that touched the depths of my soul. After hearing the words and music of that CD, I was determined to learn the Language of the Stars, so I ordered the CDs from Judy Satori that would activate that part of my Self.

I will never forget the day I first played those CDs. The voice of the great being Thoth spoke through Judy, and I sat rapt in my small office with the door shut and absorbed the energy and sounds of the strange words and tones that emanated from the CDs.

After listening for a time, I felt words coming from a deep place inside of me, but they just sat in my throat. I didn't know what to do with them; it was something I had never experienced. Finally, I began to whisper the foreign sounds. It seemed as though someone else was bringing forth those strange words that just kept bubbling up and coming out of my mouth.

We all have the beautiful, cosmic language of the stars precoded into every cell of our body, into our very DNA. We have just forgotten. That day, the energy, tones, and the words of Thoth spoken through Judy Satori activated the language I held within. I could no longer contain it. It just kept coming out of my very being and needed to be verbalized. I felt so full of all the words that they needed to spill out. And they did.

There are times when earthly language cannot properly or fully express emotions that can be expressed beautifully through Light Language. I find when I become emotional, the first language that wants to come out of me is the Language of the Stars, so sometimes I just let go and allow it, and it always feels so good.

It isn't even the words that make such an impact; it is the energy, the vibrations of the sounds. Light Language is a galactic language of love and light, a gift from Spirit, which sparks or helps to activate our dormant strands of DNA. It usually cannot be translated literally but is made up of symbols—Light-filled, sacred geometry.

My Starry side was expanding more and more. I practiced meditation daily, and through those countless meditative hours, I became more and more familiar with my true home and Starry life. I began to remember past lives, and through the remembering, I understood myself, my present life, and various situations.

Finally, everything that had always puzzled me and caused confusion was beginning to make sense. I had definitely found what was missing in my life, and that was the knowledge and richness gained from numerous incarnations on this planet and others, as well as other galaxies and universes.

One day while trolling the Internet, I came upon a website that revealed yet another part of my diverse and countless incarnations. It was a short audio clip labelled "The Chanting of the Lemurian Priestesses."

Once again, I was drawn to a new experience. As I listened to the chanting, I put my head down near my computer and absorbed the words. Suddenly, I found myself chanting along with them. I knew the chant! I knew the words! I remembered the intonation.

As I chanted, I saw myself in a vision, where I was with a group of priestesses in a circle, our arms on each other's shoulders, circling slowly in time with the chant.

We were all dressed in beautiful, long, bright red gowns. Mine was a V-neck, draped elegantly to the ground, and I was wearing a wide, gold belt that fastened just under the breast line. I had long, straight, black hair.

For those of you who have not heard of Lemuria, here is a brief description:

Both Atlantis and Lemuria were massive continents that existed on Earth approximately 26,000 years ago. Atlantis was in the Atlantic Ocean and Lemuria was in the Pacific Ocean. There is much history surrounding these two continents. The hierarchy of each was of differing opinions, and eventually they came to war with each other.

Atlantis was known as a patriarchal society and controlled by dark forces that did not wish for a peaceful planet. They wanted to control humanity at their whim, which was considered interference by the galactic community and not allowed. This did not deter the dark forces. Warfare was their game.

Lemuria was a matriarchal society that desired to allow humanity to evolve at its own pace. They were a kinder, gentler group, and many were incarnates from the Pleiades star system. The result was war and the complete destruction of both landmasses. First Lemuria sank below the waves, and then Atlantis self-destructed due to the decadence that existed there.

I do not know of any remnants of Atlantis, but there are some parts of Lemuria still above the waves: the

Hawaiian Islands, Fiji, and New Zealand. There could be more small islands that I am not aware of.

I have other memories of incarnations on Lemuria—happy times long, long ago—but I only have one memory of existing on Atlantis. There must be a good reason for that, although I do not know what it is.

TIME AND EVENTS MARCH ONWARD

Sleep time can be, and very often is, an interesting part of life, at least for the aspiring disciple. One early morning, I awoke and heard the voices of people laughing and talking. Puzzled, I got out of bed to investigate.

The house was dark and now silent. I thought maybe my husband had fallen asleep and forgotten to shut off the TV. That was not so; the TV was off. I walked around a few rooms, then reluctantly went back to bed, my many questions unanswered. I thought maybe my team of guides and angels were having a party and had neglected to invite me!

Later, I realized what had occurred. During our sleep time, we are usually very busy, as we all astral travel. I had been somewhere out in the ethers, traveling in my Lightbody, likely visiting with my star family, and my conscious mind woke a few seconds before my Lightbody returned. So, my conscious mind was aware of what my Lightbody was experiencing.

Contained within my many years traveling the path to enlightenment, I've had numerous interesting experiences, but a few are more prominent than others. One such incident is etched in my mind and surfaces occasionally.

A few years ago, I was enjoying a nice lunch with a few family members at a small restaurant that served healthy, good-tasting food. I had brought a bottle of water, as I usually do, and placed it on the table. When my visit ended, I picked up my bottle of water, put it inside my roomy purse, left the building, and walked a short distance across the parking lot to my car.

Upon reaching my car, I looked in my purse for my car keys and noticed that my water bottle was not there. When I looked inside the car, I saw my water bottle sitting nicely in the holder in the console.

Confusion set in and initially I had no idea what had happened. How could this be? My car was locked, I had just put my water bottle in my purse a few minutes prior, and now here it was, sitting inside the locked car! Spirit certainly does work in mysterious ways.

A little later, I realized what had transpired. My team had taken me on board the ship and wanted me to know that, so they brought me back a few seconds earlier in time so that I could see the water bottle in the locked car and realize that I had been gone...without even knowing it.

In the higher dimensions, there is no "time." The beings that reside in those higher dimensions have knowledge and use technology that people on this planet would find mystifying. It is all very exciting. I only wish I could have remembered that very brief time lapse when I was with my team, but that was not to be.

When we are here, incarnated within this physical body, we need to stay "grounded," and if we remember too much of being on the other side during those wonderful visits, most of us would be unable to function very well, if at all, while here.

I know now that nothing that ever happens is an accident; those kinds of experiences are given to us for a reason, and perhaps my reason was to further cement the knowledge of my Starry life deeper within my being. It worked!

I've had countless experiences along this path that I have chosen, and as it progressed, I learned a valuable lesson.

During the earlier years of my incredible journey, my joy and excitement in each situation was second to none! I wanted to tell the world about all those wonderful experiences, but that was not always wise.

There are those who are not on the same path and just do not understand, so it is futile to tell them anything. Either they won't believe you and likely think you are "woo-woo," or they are just not interested in it and would rather discuss the weather.

Whenever I was full of myself and let slip some juicy morsel relating to my journey, I was often met with ridicule, disdain, or ennui. Eventually, I learned to keep it to myself unless I was speaking with another like-minded individual. It usually is beneficial to choose our audience.

Even though it was a hard lesson for me to learn, I realized that each experience and each situation adds a richness and fullness to the journey.

SELF-HEALING

When we formulate our life plans, we can be very inventive. It often amazes me how the learning process transpires and what the results eventually are. Activity has always been a huge part of my life, and some of my many pastimes over the years have included golfing, hiking, cardio workouts involving dance steps and a dance group, jogging, walking, working out in a gym, skiing, and yoga. All that activity can cause wear and tear on the body despite keeping one relatively fit and healthy.

Those many activities are no longer on my agenda; however, I still walk each day for many reasons. Our physical bodies are very intelligent. The body will tell the mind what needs to happen regarding food, sleep, and exercise. There was a time when my body was telling me to slow down. I developed pain in my legs and hips so severe that I could not fall asleep.

My spirituality told me to call on my team of guides and angels for help, since I had no desire to make use of pharmaceuticals. My team promptly assisted. When I went to bed, my pain would get worse; I asked for help, and in about thirty seconds, I was pain-free and was able to fall asleep.

This ritual continued through the winter months in Arizona and for a short time after returning to Alberta. Then all the assistance stopped, and the pain returned. Puzzled, I went into meditation and asked, "Why?"

I was shocked at the answer.

"We gave you the tools. Use them."

As I write this, I have to smile. But at that time, my fragile feelings were hurt, and my ego went into full-blown indignation. When humans (or maybe any species) suffer an ego setback, generally the first emotion to surface is fear. Fear leads to anger, blame, and a whole lot of other negative emotions.

I felt anger. I can hardly believe that now, but at that time, anger was front and center.

How can they do this to me?
I trust them. Why aren't they helping me?
They must be punishing me for something—what could it be?
What did I do wrong?

Heavy, intense thoughts of negativity surfaced, and my emotions took a dive deep down into the proverbial rabbit hole.

Yes, I felt fear: fear of not knowing what to do, fear of the pain, fear of not sleeping, fear of maybe having to take pills filled with toxic chemicals.

And then anger reared its head, because I wanted someone else to fix my problems and they refused.

None of my emotions were good. And worst of all, my wonderful angelic group had said no to me! What a blow to my delicate ego!

After the anger came contrition—a deep sorrow and guilt, more negative emotions. I was an emotional mess. The guilt and shame I felt were worse than the pain. Then the real remorse set in, and I blamed myself.

How can I be angry at an angel?
Will they still love me and want to work with me?

I felt lost and abandoned, and that is what happens when we lose our connection to Spirit. We feel lost and alone even though we are not.

After a time, I realized the error of my ways and set about doing what I could to resolve the issue. Feeling there was no choice left, I went to a doctor, who dutifully took X-rays and showed me the result. Inflammation was present in both of my hips and the small of my back. I was told I had arthritis and would need medication to manage the pain and inflammation.

Horror stories are often rampant in circles of those who are aging, and I'd heard my share. "Well, so-and-so had arthritis and took this particular pill. She had a bad heart, and the medication was too strong for her, so she died."

I was determined that I would not take pills.

Next, I just "happened" to come across a book written by a wonderful soul named Louise Hay. The title of the book was *You Can Heal Your Life*. That book changed my life in several positive ways. After reading the book from cover to cover, I decided that if Louise Hay could heal her body, so could I heal mine!

Once again, I stepped into unfamiliar territory and went in with both feet planted firmly on the ground, with love, determination, and hope in my heart. The wonderful and amazing part of all of this is that I did have help and that help came, but only after I made the decision to help myself. At that time, I was not aware of this truth; I genuinely thought I was in the process alone, but I was determined to heal myself. And I did.

After much consideration, I developed a plan that would take me through this process of healing. My first task was to search the Internet to find out what a hip joint looked like; I needed to know so I could visualize it. That accomplished, I went into meditation and allowed my imagination to take over.

Through the magical world of imagining, I envisioned a tiny, little me, about an inch tall. In my hand, I carried a small bucket and brush. I positioned my little Self at the top of my head, opened my crown chakra, then proceeded to make my way down to the small of my back, using my spine as my ladder.

Once in the area of the inflammation, I began to use my scrub brush to remove the inflammation, and as I did so, I put it all in my bucket. You see, my Self, my bucket, and my brush were all magic.

I had the freedom to imagine myself any size I chose to, so I made a tiny me. The brush could do anything I wanted it to, and my bucket could hold as much as I put into it. The scrubbing began in my right hip joint, moved to the small of my back, and ended at the left hip joint.

When I felt I had scrubbed enough for one session, I gathered up my bucket and brush and gingerly made my way back up the spine to my crown. Waiting there were my angelic team and guides, so I dutifully handed them my bucket filled with my inflammation and asked them to transmute it all into beautiful, white Light. They complied, and the procedure was finished for that day.

The process was a meditative one that lasted about twenty minutes, and I diligently worked at reducing my pain and inflammation every day for two years. One day,

CRYSTAL CORRIDOR OF LIGHT

I realized my pain was gone. I cannot remember exactly how I decided I was finished; it all just seemed to be perfect.

My imagination and my intention had been very powerful tools! They always are, for each one of us. The problem is, very often, we forget that truth.

I was very proud of myself and told my story to the group members at our meetings, all the while feeling quite self-righteous and pleased with myself. There I was, pain-free, no medicine involved, and I had done it all by myself!

Little did I know at the time that I did not do it all by myself. I had copious amounts of help from Spirit.

Eventually, Spirit did tell me that truth, and then I needed to retell my story to my group and confess that I did indeed have help but I was not aware of it until later. That pain and inflammation have never returned, and I am still free from medication for any health issue.

Spirit will help us if it does not interfere with our life plan, but only if we take the initiative by making the first move toward helping ourselves and then following through. It is important that we demonstrate our determination to help ourselves and trust that we have the power to do that, meaning we trust in our higher power.

Making the effort and doing our due diligence does not mean that we will be pain-free or cured overnight. It may take weeks, months, or years, as in my case. It is about trust and our willingness to take responsibility for our own well-being.

That is the way Spirit works in the higher dimensions. It will not and cannot do our work for us. If it did, what would we learn? We would become totally dependent on Spirit and never become self-reliant and acquire soul growth.

THIS WRITING, THIS BOOK

To date, there has been one more significant experience on this sacred journey of mine, and that is writing this book.

Through countless hours of meditation and doing the required inner work to raise my level of consciousness, my self-confidence has increased. That inner work allowed the energetic connection to Spirit to expand, thus giving my channeling ability a boost up. Many words of wisdom have made their way to my conscious mind from Spirit, and my claircognizance and clairsentience have blossomed more fully.

Having said that, I still enjoy other talented psychics' words brought in from the higher dimensions and continue to use this gift I give myself occasionally.

During one of these sessions, for the second time in my life, I was given what I considered a proverbial bombshell. The first time was when I was informed that I was a Star person.

From out of nowhere, from the astral, from the cosmos, from the higher dimensions came these words:

"We see you writing a book."

Just those words, nothing else.

I was completely shocked and speechless. After a few moments, in a startled, high-pitched voice, I blurted out, "Me?"

More silence was the reply.

Then I continued, "I don't know anything about writing a book."

Their reply was, "Do you accept this task?"

Still feeling somewhat bewildered and overwhelmed, I said, "Yes."

Driving home from that incredible session was a very emotionally chaotic person behind the wheel. Oh, I drove just fine, but my mind was racing, and confusing thoughts bombarded my head like little, sharp bullets bouncing around. Of course, I arrived home safely and related the situation to my husband.

"I guess I'm supposed to write a book," I said.

"Oh, well, you better get started then," he said, and that was that.

My confusion at hearing the message from Spirit was due to the Veil of Forgetfulness. After the initial shock of learning about writing a book, I realized that the message was a gentle reminder. Writing this book is an important segment of my life plan that I had chosen before taking human form, and I had forgotten about it. For someone like me, who had never thought of writing a book, it was quite a shock, but I recovered and carried on with my chosen work.

For the next few months, I struggled mightily, both mentally and emotionally. I had no idea what I needed to write or how I would do it. My first feeble attempts were futile, and nothing was accomplished. After a few months of suffering through the confusion, I decided to be more pragmatic.

With much contemplation, I realized that my greatest spiritual strength lies in my knowledge of the Ancient Wisdom. I have a solid grasp on that subject. A wide perspective. So, that was step number one.

Then, the next questions were: What shall I do with that knowledge? What am I good at? What talent do I have that I am able to give to others? My answer was: I am a teacher. A teacher of the Ancient Wisdom. It is what I've been doing for the past ten years.

"Okay, there you have it," I said to myself. "Do something with it." Step number two.

And so, this book was born.

My journey has continued to progress, to evolve, as have I: hosting more classes, writing more blogs, meeting more wonderful, like-minded souls who would gift me with their presence at my meetings, thus enriching my life even more. And now this book exists, my life experiences compiled within these pages.

I love my work. I love my mission. I love my life.

Archangel Michael's Message

Deep within your subconscious mind
lies the truth of who you are and from whence you came.
The shrouding of the Veil thins, causing
faint stirrings of awakening,
and a restlessness begins that the Soul cannot deny.

Echoes of ancient civilizations dance
across your consciousness
and distant memories of past lives
on many planets, galaxies, and universes surface.

These memories of rich and varied experiences
open a doorway into the vast unknown
and set you upon the Path to Enlightenment.

~ Channeled by Bethel

———

Who are we?

Where are we from?

Why are we here?

Questions are an excellent way to learn. Being curious about life, about anything and everything, is good because it means we will search for the answers, and when we discover the answers, we gain more knowledge. Knowledge enables us to understand the world around us, and when we understand, we are better equipped to accept others, our surroundings, and our circumstances.

Those who have questions are seeking answers; therefore, they are a Seeker. A Seeker of truth. Their task, then, is to discern what is truth and what is not. That ability lies in the heart, for that is where all the answers, truth, and power reside.

*W*ho Are We?

S ource energy. Prime Creator. The One of all that is.
The great Being is known by many names. The
Being is energy. It is a Great Consciousness, the most
powerful force in Creation. It *is* Creation and does not
Itself take physical form.

In order to experience Itself, Source radiated forth
fragments, or sparks of Itself, and those sparks are souls,
all children of the Creator—all created equally—and are
eternal Beings of Light. We are those sparks of Light. We
are a consciousness. We are all one with Source.

Source is comprised of equal parts of feminine and
masculine energy. The Mother (feminine) part holds the
matter, the "mater," and is the giver of birth. The Father
(masculine) part is the ignition, the switch, the Light that
lit the "mater" and began the consciousness. The Mother
is the planner, and the Father is the One who carries out
the plan.

We, too, as souls, hold equal parts of feminine and masculine energy, the same components as Source. When we were birthed from the "mater," we were given the gift of free will to go forth and experience life in all forms and realities, with no judgment from anyone, including Source. Source does not judge. Source creates.

Where Are We From?

We are from everywhere and nowhere. We are eternal. We are from the stars, from the cosmos, from the omniverse. We have lived on countless planets and in many galaxies and universes. Perhaps our most recent choice of star system to inhabit was the Pleiades, Arcturus, Orion, Lyra, Sirius, Andromeda, or one of a myriad of others.

Why Are We Here?

The main reason many souls choose to be here at this time in the history of Earth is to ascend while occupying the physical body. Not everyone who is here at this time has chosen to ascend. It is not a requirement; it is a choice. Ascension is not a place to go; it is a level of consciousness. We choose to reach a fifth dimensional level of awareness while in the physical, as a collective.

It is a grand endeavor that has never before been attempted in our galaxy and is a monumental step up in evolution for all of humanity. When I say "as a collective," that does not mean every soul inhabiting the planet; it means just enough people waking up and remembering the truth in order to achieve a "tipping point" to enable the mass ascension.

Understanding why we choose to ascend in this way requires some background information. Planet Earth was birthed by the Divine Mother to be a Garden of

Eden, a lush planet rich in resources and a place of great beauty.

It was designed to be a playground for the angels, where they could assume physicality and experience all the gifts Earth had to offer. It began as a fifth dimensional planet, and the consciousness of Earth was, and still is, Archangel Ariel (Gaia), the Mother Goddess of our universe.

Due to free will, humanity made choices that were more of "service to self" than "service to others," such as greed, wars, desire for power, lack of love and compassion. All the negative energy from those actions and emotions caused Earth to slowly descend in density from the fifth level to the third.

This means that the vibrational frequency (the rate of speed) of humanity's physical bodies slowed due to the abuse and oppression of a malevolent, extraterrestrial force that was present on and around our planet.

When the vibrational frequency of humanity's bodies slowed, most fell in dimension (level of awareness), but there were some who were able to keep their God spark shining brightly enough to remember the truth of who we really are and where we come from. Those few were able to keep their level of awareness in the fourth or fifth dimension.

The oppression and abuse have held us all captive through our own thoughts, words, and deeds. The density we created caused many to lose sight of the Light within, meaning we forgot our connection to Creator. When that happened, Gaia chose to move down to the third density with humanity and then from there, as a collective, move back up to the fifth dimension (level of awareness) in a mass ascension. That is what is currently occurring on our planet.

The souls that are here now volunteered for the opportunity to be a part of this great ascension because of the existing situation in our world, a situation so dire that the planet is close to destruction caused by eons of negativity and abuse. Archangel Gaia said, "Enough. Change must happen for the survival of Earth and humanity." And so it is.

Change is indeed happening, and we all have front-row seats. We volunteered, but we were also *chosen*. We were chosen because we are experienced, seasoned souls. We have endured countless lifetimes here and never gave up; we kept coming back to aid in the liberation, and that liberation is transpiring as I write this.

There were other reasons for coming here, one of which is that we have the opportunity to take a huge leap forward in evolution just by being here and working toward our freedom.

We can do this by:

- Learning lessons: Earth is a planet where there is great opportunity to learn and grow spiritually, because life here can be very difficult. When faced with challenges, the objective is to use our free will to act or react in a positive way. Choosing love, compassion, acceptance, and understanding will allow us to advance in evolution. When we come from the lower vibrations such as anger, fear, or judgment, we do not advance spiritually.

- Clearing karma: When we inhabit a planet, we often create a situation where there is negative energy that cannot be cleared in the higher dimensions; it must be cleared where it was created. There is no rule or law forcing a soul to clear karma. It is a soul choice. If karma is not cleared, the negativity can impede spiritual advancement, so usually the soul decides to deal with it.

- Performing service to others: This can be accomplished in a variety of ways—healing modalities, volunteering, and teaching are just a few. There are souls who help others just by "being," and in this way, they send out their loving, kind energy to all they come in contact with.

Occasionally, a soul will choose to incarnate with a severe disability or alcohol or drug addiction to teach others compassion and acceptance. There are also times when a soul will assume physical form just for the experience.

What Is a Starseed?

A Starseed is just that, a soul from another star system that is seeded onto a planet, one who has the desire to experience life in many different realities and forms. They are explorers and adventurers eager to learn and move on up the ladder of evolution. Many come in with the purpose of helping others, and there are those who just wish to experience life.

We are eternal beings; our souls are eternal. In our purest form, we are Light, Love/Light, as it is with our Source. The way in which we experience life in all realities and in all forms is to incarnate, to become physical, to have a body.

There is much thought and preparation involved when planning an incarnation. It is a very complicated and wide-ranging process involving many other souls that are part of the soul family and soul group.

Agreements must be formulated with each one who will be a part of the journey. The Earth parents, siblings, mate, friends, and various extended family members are chosen with great care.

Body type and physical traits are preplanned, and everything and everyone pertaining to the complex journey are carefully selected. All must be in total agreement before the incarnation begins. We also choose the karma we wish to clear or balance (if any), the lessons we want to learn, and the growth that is desired.

When all the preparation is complete, the final project is then presented to the Council of Twelve for their endorsement. The soul agreement is a sacred contract and adhered to with great respect by the Beings in the higher dimensions.

We do not do this alone. We have help from many— our soul family, our soul group, our guides, and various higher dimensional councils, priests, and priestesses. It is a complicated, precise process. When we are ready, we are given a blessing and sent forth into the reality of choice.

A major part of the criteria for having an incarnation is that we must take the Veil of Forgetfulness, meaning we are obliged to forget who we are and where we are from, forget our Starry life and our loved ones we leave behind. If we retained full memory of those in the higher dimensions, our journeys would be nigh impossible to complete, and our yearning for our true home would supersede our desire to complete the incarnation. So, we must forget. Also, if we remembered all that we knew while we lived on the "other side," what would we learn here?

Some souls come in choosing a short time of forgetfulness, and there are those who live the life, transition to the higher dimensions from whence they came without ever piercing the Veil, never remembering their life in the Stars. It is a soul choice.

When we take the Veil of Forgetfulness, there is a backup plan put into place. When we decide to experience an incarnation, we place only a small portion of ourselves into a physical body. The greater part of the soul stays back, becomes the director of the journey, and is the major guide during the life stream. This being is known as our Higher Self.

The life we choose can be whatever we want it to be. It can be a short incarnation, or we can choose to live a long life, one of luxury or poverty, good health or chronic illness.

Our choices are limitless. We have the free will to wear a dark hat or a white hat. There is no judgment in the higher dimensions; there is no right or wrong. Everything just is. Everyone plays a role for their own reasons, and all choices are accepted.

During the incarnation, we are assisted by numerous Beings of Light. We have our very own guardian angel who never, ever leaves us; he or she is our constant companion throughout our lifetime. And there are guides and angels who come and go during our journey and can be either male or female.

The Incarnation

Once we are birthed, we connect with and adjust to the energy of the planet we are about to inhabit and begin our incredible journey. In infancy, our energy is very close to Source, and the Veil is not completely drawn. We have the ability to see our guides and angels. That is why infants often appear to be staring fixedly, seeing something that we do not see. The "forgetting" occurs gradually, as we become conditioned to life as a human.

Many young children have an "invisible friend," a companion, someone they comfortably interact with through conversation and games. Adults tend to discount this as imagination, but to the child, it is real. Some children see spirits in their bedroom, and when they tell their parents, they are frequently told to "quit imagining and go to sleep." Eventually, the child begins to believe it is their imagination and shut themselves off from this great gift. A few stands staunch in their truth and continue to interact with the world of Spirit.

Whether a child continues to see and communicate with the Spirit world depends on the soul choice. Some never forget, and others completely forget and never experience that world again. Most commonly, as children, we see and know the outer world, then through conditioning such as acquiring a religious belief, attending an educational facility, experiencing peer pressure, and being part of a society that often discounts the metaphysical, we do forget. Many will return to the metaphysical, their outer world, later in life, at a time that is determined preincarnate.

The Call of the Soul

E ach soul's journey is different and unique to that soul. It is all preplanned and precisely guided. Since the goal of humanity and that of Archangel Gaia—the consciousness of this planet—is to ascend together, most disciples choose to have a designated time when they will awaken to the truth of who they are and from whence they came.

There is no set time for those incarnated to awaken. It is different for each one. It can be as children, teens, young adults, or elders. It is all a preincarnate soul choice. In the group meetings that I have hosted for about ten years, I have had participants as young as ten and as old as eighty.

The call of the soul comes from the Higher Self and can arrive in a variety of ways. Spirit is very innovative. Then, the disciple's task is to listen to the call and move forward on the spiritual path. The Higher Self may use one or more of a variety of ways to alert the disciple that it is time for the awakening to begin. These are often referred to as synchronicities. The universe loves synchronicities.

The following are some examples of synchronicities:

- A familiar scent may be present for no apparent reason and continue for several days, months, or even years. It often is a floral scent, sometimes woodsmoke.

- A set of number sequences may show up regularly, often on license plates and billboards.

- The disciple may hear their name called, but there is no one else in the room.

- The same color may be seen repeatedly, and this color may have special meaning for the soul that no one else is aware of.

- A song that has special meaning to the disciple may be heard regularly on the radio.

- A certain streetlight may go off and on each time one walks under it. Spirit often works with electricity to attract the attention of a disciple.

- If in a library searching for a solution to a particular problem or question, a disciple might be drawn to a certain book, or it might even fall off the shelf in front of them! This has happened to more than one dedicated Seeker.

All these incidents can cause confusion and raise questions that sometimes prod the soul to dig deeper, to try to find out what is really happening. Occasionally, the gentle prodding is ignored.

The incarnate, using their free will, have the choice to explore the call or disregard it and continue with their focus on Earthly life. When and if that happens, there is no judgment from anyone in the higher realms. We are all eternal beings and have eternity to evolve.

When one hears the call of the soul, then heeds that call and begins the journey to enlightenment, for many, there is no turning back—it is undeniable. There is a hunger, a yearning that compels the soul ever onward, and this is when the disciple becomes a true Seeker, and that role dominates the Seeker for the remainder of the incarnation.

There are occasionally souls who begin the path of a Seeker, then stop. Often, it is because Earth life takes precedence or circumstances arise that sway the Seeker back to a life they are more familiar with or adapted to.

For those who continue to heed the call of their Higher Self, the journey then becomes a series of un-raveling mysteries, of opening doors and exploring every nook and cranny before moving on to the next door for the delights that can be found therein, forever going forward into the World of Spiritualism.

What is Spiritualism?

Spiritualism is being connected to God, nature, each other, and the deepest part of ourselves (going within and finding the God spark that exists there) and really discovering who we are. It is being comfortable in one's own skin, being our own best friend and liking ourselves.

It is knowing that we on planet Earth do not have a monopoly on life, knowing that there are countless Beings residing in the cosmos in many different star systems and universes.

It is the knowledge that we are all here to learn and evolve on our way back to our Source.

It is being able to connect with God through our hearts without going through a middleman or woman. A very effective way to do this is through the meditation process.

It is knowing Prime Creator without the aid of organized religion.

It is a practice that goes beyond religion. Spirituality embraces all religions but is not bound to any one religious faith or belief.

It is where we are in harmony with the universe and nature, where we honor all life forms, knowing we are not above any life form because we are all One.

It is realizing that everything is energy.

It is a belief in angelic guides, meditation, reincarnation, karma, yoga, and natural healing methods, to name a few.

It is the knowledge that we can literally "heal our life," that we have the ability and the power to heal ourselves—physically, mentally, and emotionally.

It is using our psychic abilities freely and without fear.

It is knowing that a spiritual approach to God is through love, where there is no judgment, only acceptance.

Spiritualism is being able to look at another human and preceive the soul that dwells within the physical body instead of just seeing the body.

It is a magical world of dancing with the faeries, playing with the gnomes, laughing with the sprites, seeing beauty in everything and everyone. The incredible colors of the natural world become more vibrant, and one becomes aware of the glorious design and perfection of Creation.

The Healing Power of Mother Earth

Someone once asked me, "If the weather is gray, and rainy, are there higher levels of negative energy?"

My answer was that the negative energy we sometimes experience during this kind of weather rises from within, and we have the power to change that to positive energy in various ways.

Walking outdoors is therapeutic to me. I will most often connect with nature, and making that connection is very healing. Often, the walks are a meditation. Occasionally, I will receive messages from the higher dimensions, and the result is clarity, peace, and rejuvenation for my soul. It is a time for me to feel and express gratitude for the opportunity to be here at this time in the history of the planet, gratitude for those times when I feel rewarded for something, and gratitude for the times when I struggle, as those times are when I learn and gain soul growth.

My walks are an opportunity to really focus on my thoughts, words, deeds, and emotions, to focus on the energy that I put out into my surroundings. To think about focusing on my "now" and doing what I can do to create my own positive reality, to create the kind of world I want to live in.

Connecting with the earth is always beneficial to our mental, emotional, physical, and spiritual well-being. Notice the landscape as you walk. Most any area of the globe has an abundance of natural beauty.

In the province of Alberta, where I spend my summers, clover in bloom is plentiful, and I bring my attention to those lovely, dainty little florets. Then there are the wild roses so abundant in the prairie summer. Their scent is delicate and pleasant, and I often stop for a moment to poke my nose into a pink bloom to inhale the fragrance.

I suggest that if you can find a green space—most cities and towns have them—you should walk through and pay attention to what nature has to offer.

There are jackrabbits bounding along, their big ears so prominent, they make me chuckle.

The spruce and pine trees are abundant and sprouting new growth.

After a rain shower during the night, the morning air smells so fresh and sweet. Listen to the chirping of the birds; their morning songs vary as they give us a concert of harmonious sound.

Sometimes we are gifted with the aroma of freshly cut grass.

Notice the various shades of green as you walk along—so many different hues of so many different plants, yet all melds perfectly, as intended by Creator.

Sometimes I enjoy a morning walk in the rain. I can take an umbrella or not; it's only water and my clothes will dry. It is very refreshing to feel the rain on my face and to enjoy the smell of the earth as she is washed and nourished.

Our beloved Mother Earth is an amazing healer. She will raise our vibration when we walk upon her by just "being." The healing power of the earth is ours if we choose to acknowledge it and make use of it. Mother Earth is generous as well as beautiful! We can give back to her by intentionally gifting her with our Light as we take each step. I like to thank Mother Earth for her love, her beauty, and her bounty.

Déjà Vu, Precognition, and the Four Clairs of Intuition

My first peek at the paranormal was when I was a child of about eight years. I saw my guardian angel in the forest as she moved from one tree to another. She presented herself as an adult-sized, dense, gray shadow. As a young child, I did not know what I had seen, but I never forgot it. That incident is as real to me today as it was then.

Years later, when I was in my early twenties, I experienced déjà vu and precognition. These amazing experiences puzzled me, raised many unanswered questions, and firmly set me on the path of a true Seeker. The following is what I learned.

Déjà Vu—The literal meaning is "already seen."

The Wikipedia definition is: "...when a person has done something and they experience the same feelings or feeling that one has lived through the present situation before."

The situation that I saw and experienced at that time was my remembrance of the preparation of that particular situation while formulating my life plan preincarnate.

The remembrance was a message from my Higher Self saying, "You are on the right path, exactly where you need to be at this moment in time."

Precognition—Knowledge of an event that has yet to occur. A premonition of a future incident or development.

I just knew the phone was going to ring and who would be on the other end. I knew my good friend was about to knock on the door before the knock came.

Clairvoyance—Clear seeing. Seeing images or events with the third eye, the pineal gland. Can be either in our head as a vision or in front of our body.

Clairaudience—Clear hearing. Hearing a voice either in your head or as if someone is standing right beside you and speaking.

Clairsentience—Clear feeling. Recognizing the energy or emotions and feelings of another person, room, situation, or area.

Claircognizance—Clear knowing. Knowing something without reading the information or without someone relating the information to you.

These psychic gifts can surface at any time in our life, and it all happens when our Higher Self deems the time is right and we are ready for a particular experience. Our sacred journeys can be compared to a flower unfolding; nothing can be rushed. It all needs to occur naturally.

We are usually given information or an experience, then a pause, and this is when we process and digest the information. It is our "still" time. We are only given as much as we can hold and process at that time in our journey. The information or experience will match the level of consciousness in which we are presently existing.

Information is often given to us as a download, where it sits nestled in our subconscious mind until we are ready to process it. All those decisions are under the direction of our Higher Self.

In my early years of searching for answers, I decided to begin the practice of meditation. For someone who had never meditated, it was confusing and seemed very difficult. I persevered, and now meditation is a huge part of my life. It is a wonderful and effective way to connect with Spirit, to connect with the Higher Self, the angels, archangels, ascended masters, or any Being of Light in the higher dimensions. Further on in this book, I have written more in depth about the practice of meditation.

Learning How to Connect with Your Angels and Guides

E veryone has a team of angels and guides that are always available. They do not interfere with our free will, but they do help us whenever they can. That means they will assist us without breaking the Universal Law of Noninterference. Their help is amplified when we reach out to them. All we need to do is hold the intention to make that connection, then ask. It is so simple, yet so profound. Once you have become aware of them and willingly allowed them into your life in a conscious manner, the feelings of love, belonging, and happiness you will experience are second to none.

When we connect with the higher dimensions and then ask for help in solving a particular problem or situation, there are times when we are denied that assistance because it could interfere in the life path; it could infringe on a lesson we chose to learn by ourselves preincarnate and thus change the outcome. We are not aware of everything we planned to accomplish while in the physical, but our team knows our life plan down to the last, tiny detail.

There are times when we may think if we ask, the answer or solution will come instantly. That is not always the case; it may not happen for a few weeks, months, or even years. Everything that happens during our lifetime is planned and directed with precision. Patience is often required, as well as acceptance of the outcome.

I've been working with my team for many years, and it is a blessing like none other. They are always there when I need help, companionship, or just someone to talk to. A Starseed's path can be very lonely at times, and that is when the guides and angels are there for us and prop us up by just being there or by perhaps gifting us with a message of love and encouragement.

There are a variety of ways to become aware of their presence. Sometimes, it is a "knowing," a feeling of just knowing what to do in a particular circumstance. Sometimes, we will receive an answer to a question we have been pondering via a conversation with someone, or maybe an answer will come in a song that we hear.

The method my team used to get my attention many years ago was blinking streetlights as I walked under them. One light would go off every time I walked under it. At that time in my life, I was not aware of who it was. I just knew it was Spirit. Once I caught on to what was really happening, my team used the streetlights to give me messages, causing the light to blink off and on in a sequence. I would write it down, then rush home to look up the meaning of the series of blinks. It was a wonderful and exciting experience!

One of Spirit's favorite ways of contacting a disciple is through a lovely, floral scent. You may also feel or sense a featherlight touch on your cheek or a feeling of something or someone gently touching your hair. It's important to express gratitude to your team, and respect is always the order of the day. If you don't receive a sign, then that too is important. It is a message that the time is not quite right. So don't get discouraged. Keep asking!

Some Seekers use the practice of automatic writing to access the higher dimensions. It is easy and effective. Just hold the intention to make the connection, and mentally ask with great respect that they work with you as you write.

Allow yourself to relax and then just start writing whatever comes to mind. This can be done anytime or after a meditation, when you are still "in the zone." In some cases, the handwriting begins to change, or you might feel an energy moving through or around you. It is important to remember when working with the Beings of Light that they will never cause fear in any way. Their messages are always encouraging and filled with love and support.

Your team members do have a great sense of humor and might even have fun with you by playing games, making your paper move, or even causing your pen or pencil to drop. They are very inventive and love to laugh! If you are not sure if you have connected, ask them for a sign, then trust in the outcome and be open to whatever comes your way. It could be a sequence of numbers such as:

- 222—Newly planted ideas are beginning to grow into reality.
- 333—The Ascended Masters are near, wanting you to know that you have their help, love, and companionship.
- 444—The angels are surrounding you now, reassuring you of their love and help.
- 555—A major change is coming to your life.

The angels will also give you messages in a combination of two or more numbers. For example:

- 1s and 2s such as 112 or 121—Your thoughts are like seeds beginning to sprout.
- 1s and 5s such as 115 or 551—Your thoughts are creating changes in your life.

Each combination or sequence has a special meaning. There are books on these numbers that can also be found online. So, if you notice recurring numbers, pay attention.

How to Meditate and the Benefits of Meditation

Meditation is both simple and more challenging than most people think. It requires focus, belief, and intention. For those who are just beginning the practice of meditation, here are some guidelines:

1. Find a place that feels quiet and peaceful.
2. Start out slowly, perhaps five to ten minutes.
3. Wear comfortable clothing, nothing restrictive.
4. You can sit in a chair with your feet on the floor, lie down, sit cross-legged, or even kneel—whatever feels most comfortable to you.
5. The room can be dark or light, depending on your preference.
6. You can set the stage using a candle, or not.

7. Begin by setting an intention about who you would like to communicate with or what you wish to accomplish by meditation.

8. Focus on your breath, follow your breath for a few minutes, take a deep breath in, then slowly exhale. Notice the sensation of the air going in your nostrils and down to your lungs or abdomen. Notice your exhalation.

9. Be kind to yourself if your mind wanders; gently bring your focus back to the breath. Don't judge yourself; no meditation is good or bad. Even if you just sit and relax, you have accomplished something—relaxation.

10. You can use guided meditations, and there are many to be found.

11. If it feels like it's time to stop, do so regardless of what the clock says.

12. Have no expectations; just allow yourself to be open and relaxed.

13. You may not receive anything from Spirit in the beginning. It's a process, a training, a way to train your mind to focus, a way to feel peace and relaxation. It is a way to activate a particular state of consciousness.

There are numerous benefits of meditating.

Meditation:

- can be done anywhere,
- requires no special clothing,
- improves sleep by helping you learn to relax,
- reduces stress,
- lowers blood pressure,
- lessens anxiety,
- offers more feelings of well-being,
- lowers heart rate,
- improves blood circulation,
- lengthens attention span,
- changes the structure of the brain (increases gray matter), and
- can help control pain and addiction by the power of intention.

Best of all, meditation is a wonderful way to quiet the mind and connect with Spirit. This happens through the intention and the belief that you will connect.

Dreams and Our Sleep Time

Many people associate sleep time with dreams, and that is good. We do dream, all of us. Sometimes we remember the dreams, and sometimes we just have a faint memory of going somewhere or being with someone.

Everyone dreams, and dreams can be puzzling, happy, or scary. Dreams cannot be taken literally; they are given to us by Spirit as messages. Even though there are often many others in your dream—sometimes people you know—everyone in the dream is an aspect of yourself.

For example, if you dream you are running from someone, you are running from yourself. There is something within yourself that lies buried, dormant, or hidden deep that you are reluctant to deal with, and you are running from that truth or situation.

If you dream you have a newborn baby, it most often means new beginnings are in your near future. If you dream you are riding a bicycle or motorcycle, it means you need more balance in your life in some area. These are just a few examples. There are many resources available online and in books if you are interested in more information on deciphering dreams.

Dreams are a way for Spirit to teach us, a way to remind us of unfinished business, a way to help us grow, or perhaps a gentle nudge to get moving on a situation that is holding us back from spiritual advancement. A good way to remember your dreams is to keep a journal by your bedside and then write down as much of the dream as you can remember as soon as you wake up.

There is a difference between a dream and a visitation. A dream is a message from your Higher Self. A visitation is a real visit from a transitioned soul, usually a loved one who has crossed over and then returned in spirit to give a message or just to say "I love you" in a way you will recognize. Both of my parents have returned in spirit to give me a message of love. I am very fortunate to have had those experiences, but, as it is with most experiences, it was a preplanned soul choice by all concerned.

There is much more than dreams happening when we sleep. It is only our conscious mind that sleeps; our Lightbody—our soul—can be, and most often is, very busy. We all do what is called astral travel, where our soul/Lightbody leaves the physical body and travels about.

Numerous occurrences unfold through our nighttime. We will often go to another part of our world to assist someone. I had a vision years ago of flying over New York City and seeing the holiday lights on the street corners. It was the month of December, and when I woke up, I knew I had gone to a strife-ridden area of one of the Southern states where there was a lot of turmoil.

Another time, I had a vision of sitting near a child and stroking his forehead. He had a shock of long, black hair, and I knew he was ill, so I was comforting him. He didn't know I was there, but perhaps he felt the feather-light touch of a soft hand on his brow and felt the comfort of my energetic being.

There are times when we astral travel and our Lightbody returns a nanosecond after our conscious mind wakes up, and that is when we hear voices and maybe just hear the end of a conversation and wonder who we were talking with. That has happened to me many times, and it happened just recently. In the past, I would have been confused, but now that I am more aware of the metaphysical world, I celebrate it!

$\mathcal{P}ast\ Lives$

Our sleep time is an excellent time for us to remember past lives. Our Higher Self will bring to the forefront of our consciousness any past life that requires attention—perhaps some unfinished or unbalanced karma. Meditation is another modality that is most useful in delving into the unknown world of past lives. I can remember a few parts of my past lives, and those memories are very special to me.

Just think of it! Maybe in some lifetime you were a queen, a king, a pauper, or a Native American. Maybe you were General Custer! Perhaps you were a samurai in Japan or a pharaoh in Egypt. Or a druid witch dancing around a huge boiling pot, throwing the eye of newt into your magical potion.

The mind and our imagination know no bounds. When incarnating, we can wear any "hat" we choose in order to experience life in all forms and realities. It really is quite amazing! Your sister could have been your mother in another life, your aunt could have been your best friend, and in this lifetime, you have things to resolve with that soul. Karma? Perhaps.

It is all contained within the magical, mystical world of the Great Unknown, and that Great Unknown is what you as a dedicated Seeker are here to explore. It's exciting, eye-opening—as in third eye—and a huge learning time to move forward in evolution.

Past lives are very meaningful because we are the product of every incarnation, experience, situation, and event we have ever faced since our soul was first cast by Source energy. This present lifetime is a culmination of every incarnation we've chosen over time, and that is one reason why it's so important to recognize the truth of who we are and where we come from. That truth is a requirement if the choice is to ascend this time around.

$\mathcal{A}$scension vs. Transition

WHAT IS ASCENSION?

Ascension is a path—the path of evolution. We are constantly evolving. That is the nature of the soul. We are forever striving to reach or become closer to our Source, and the only way to do that is to raise our consciousness. That process takes eons, and since we are timeless, immortal beings, we have lots of time to experience a variety of realities along the path.

Some of us contracted to ascend during this lifetime, and some did not. One is not better than the other, only different.

Ascension is not a place to go; it is a level of consciousness, a state of being.

It means that we reach at least a fifth-dimensional level of consciousness.

When we refer to "ascending in the physical," that represents attaining the fifth-dimensional level of consciousness or above while still inhabiting our physical body and without going through the "dying process."

We are multidimensional beings and have ascended numerous times during various lifetimes on several dimensions, planets, galaxies, and universes. We chose to ascend with Gaia and the collective on this planet at this time. We are constantly evolving and ascending, and this will never end, as we are eternal beings.

WHAT IS TRANSITION?

Transition indicates change. The word "transition" is often used in the spiritual world instead of the word "death," as "death" holds an energy of fear of the unknown for some people. Death of the physical body happens when we have completed our incarnation and go home to our families in the stars.

We don't die, only our physical body does. Our soul is eternal. We are not our body; we are our soul.

Our physical body is the vehicle we chose to use while on this planet in this lifetime. It houses our soul, which requires a physical "house" during an incarnation.

A few truths regarding ascension and transition:

- A soul may ascend without transitioning.
- A soul may transition without ascending.
- A soul may ascend and transition at the same time.

The two events are not necessarily synonymous.

The Flower Unfolds

As we continue our pursuit of knowledge, our physical, emotional, mental, and spiritual bodies begin to change. It can be compared to a metamorphosis, like a butterfly going through the various stages of life.

Some of the early indicators of these adjustments in the physical body include a change in appetite. Foods like meat, dairy, eggs, and highly processed foods can cause digestive discomfort. There can be an aversion to those that were once desired; alcoholic drinks often cannot be tolerated. Fruits, vegetables, and many plant-based foods replace the highly processed ones, as the disciple craves healthier foods. A disciple may lose or gain weight, and sleeplessness or the desire for more sleep may happen. Excess noise can cause major discomfort for some people.

The human body is smart, smarter than the mind that most often controls it. The body knows how to keep itself in good working order. The body is not who you are;

it is the vessel the soul chose to navigate the journey. It "houses" the soul, and that is why it is so important to take good care of it. The soul itself cannot have an incarnation. It needs a physical vessel to hold it, to carry it through the lifetime.

The emotional body also undergoes massive shifts: interests change, people who were once considered good friends no longer resonate energetically, relationships can fall by the wayside, and job changes often occur. A goal to balance the masculine and feminine energies becomes important.

The pineal gland begins to awaken as the shrouding of the Veil lifts: psychic abilities surface, dreams may be more vivid, paranormal experiences are presented to the disciple, the intuition grows stronger, and messages from the higher dimensions come more often and with greater clarity. Images of spirits may be seen either with the physical eyes or with the third eye, the pineal gland.

The disciple seeks out groups of like-minded people and will often attend various classes looking for answers. An interest in natural healing often develops, and these areas of health care are often utilized instead of relying solely on medical workers and pharmaceuticals.

The urge to become a practitioner in the healing modalities such as meditation, massage, and Reiki, may arise. New Age establishments pique the interest, and all the treasures within those stores, such as crystals, candles, incense, meditation music, icons, and essential oils, are explored. Massive lifestyle changes abound!

The Starseed Highway is such an incredible, amazing, exciting road! As the Seeker moves along from one cycle or phase to another, each step brings clarity and often more questions. It's comparable to opening doors. Open a door, explore the new surroundings, gain clarity, then move on to the next room and explore that one, and so on. More questions bring more searching and more rich and exciting experiences.

As we learn and grow spiritually, we are constantly changing, and these changes nudge us ever forward. Soon, we are probing the mysterious world of the chakras and auras.

The Chakras

What are they?
What do they do?

How do they affect our journey?

We have a physical body, but we also have an energetic body. Our physical body is the vessel that houses the soul. The energetic body *is* the soul. It is the *prana* or life force within us, within the physical vessel. It is comprised of our consciousness, chakras, kundalini, and the auric field.

There are seven main chakras and many smaller ones that can be recognized as a myriad of life streams that run throughout the human vessel. In the ancient language of India (Sanskrit), the word "chakra" means "wheel" or "disk."

Chakras are energy centers within the physical body, and each one corresponds to specific nerves and organs. All the chakras hold and conduct energy, and each has a distinct purpose that is designed to keep the physical body in good working condition. Each chakra is a certain color.

The chakras take in energy from the outside world, bringing needed life essence to all the body organs. These energy centers affect all four of our bodies—spiritual, emotional, mental, and physical—meaning whatever is happening within our bodies regarding our thoughts and feelings is reflected by the chakras.

When we are calm, at peace, and happy, the chakras work efficiently and perfectly. When there is an issue with one or more of our four bodies, the chakras become sluggish and do not work as well. For example, if we are unhappy and feel depressed, angry, or anxious, those emotions will affect our organs and cause a variety of physical problems, including lowering our immune system, thereby making us vulnerable to disease and pain.

The three lower chakras are root, sacral, and solar plexus. These three lower chakras pertain to the physical part of life. The three upper ones are throat, third eye, and crown, and they assume responsibility for the spiritual aspect of the journey. The heart chakra lies in the center of the upper and lower chakras and acts as the bridge between the physical and the spiritual.

1. Root chakra—Ruby red in color. The root chakra is related to our survival and grounding, the will to live, and everything that makes the body feel

safe and secure, such as food, shelter, and money. It is located at the base of the spine. It is closest to the earth and helps keep us grounded. This chakra supports the spinal column, kidneys, bones, and muscles.

2. Sacral chakra—Orange in color. The sacral chakra is our emotional identity, our giving and receiving, creativity, passion, and sexuality. It is located just below the navel. It works with the ovaries, testes, and immune system.

3. Solar plexus—Yellow in color. The solar plexus chakra is where our power lies, our core strength, our willpower. It relates to our self-determination, motivation, goals, control, and freedom. This chakra works with our pancreas, stomach, gall bladder, and small intestine, and it is situated just below the rib cage in the diaphragm area.

4. Heart chakra—Green in color. It is the link between the three lower and the three upper chakras. It is where and how we connect the physical (the three lower chakras) with the spiritual (the three upper chakras). The heart chakra is where our compassion, acceptance, and love of self and others lie. It is the center of harmony, peace, and balance and works as a "cleaner" of negative energy of self or others. This chakra takes

care of the circulatory system, heart, thymus, and upper back.

5. Throat chakra—Blue in color. This chakra is our communication center, the center of self-expression, our truth, and how we represent ourselves to the outer world. It supports the thyroid, lungs, esophagus, bronchi, and throat.

6. Third eye chakra—Indigo in color. It is located between the eyebrows and is the center of our awareness, insight, intuition, visions, and wisdom. It supports the pituitary gland, pineal gland, ears, and nervous system.

7. Crown chakra—Some recognize it as violet, others as white or a combination of both. The crown chakra is the chakra of spiritual expression, awakening, and our connection to the spiritual world. It is our universal identity, our cosmic consciousness, the center of our I AM Presence. It is where we work from to expand our consciousness. It is located on the top of our head, our crown.

Because the chakras affect our lives in every way, it is important to keep them clear, clean, and balanced. There are a variety of methods we can use to keep our energetic body in good operating order, such as meditation, intention, and visualization.

Clear and Balance the Chakras

L ight is the manifestation that holds the closest vibration to Source, and water is the second. Using light to clean and clear the chakras is simple and effective. Whenever a Starseed works on the inner self, it is always a good idea to call in Spirit. Call on your Higher Self, your team of angels and guides, or any specific angel you feel comfortable with.

Then, hold the intention to open the crown chakra and imagine a glorious beam of white light coming down from the heavens into the crown and slowly going through the chakras, cleaning and clearing each one. There is no limit to what you can do; it is whatever you imagine it to be. Be inventive!

You can visualize the white light collecting everything that is not in your highest and best good as it progresses down to your foot chakras and out into the earth, as deep as you wish, where it will be transformed by Mother Earth into beautiful, golden light.

Water is another powerful tool to use in the chakra cleansing process. When you're in the shower, connect with Spirit and imagine the water flowing over you, cleansing each chakra. starting at the crown. Hold the intention that whatever is not for your highest and best good is being washed down the drain to be transmuted by Mother Earth.

A good way to balance and align the chakras is, while in meditation, imagine each of your seven main chakras about the size of a basketball. Next, set them one on top of another in a perfect column, making sure they are all the same size. Then, visualize a beam of white light coming down into the crown chakra and going in a straight line through the chakras, bringing them into perfect alignment.

There are numerous ways to clear, balance, and align the chakras, and these are just a few. It is important to use the tools that you find most effective and that you are most comfortable with.

$\mathcal{T}$he Aura

The aura is an energy field that surrounds anything that has a vibration, such as the moon, planets, humans, animals, plants, and crystals. Some people can see it with the physical eyes, but that may take practice.

The human aura is a multilayered field of living light that surrounds the body and is composed of information from every cell in the body. It has seven layers that correspond to the seven chakras.

These two forces of life essence affect each other, and one is an indication of the other. The aura is the body's external energy, while the chakras are the internal energy. Each band of energy has a different color, vibrates at a different frequency, and corresponds with a specific chakra.

The aura is your energetic space. It is the exterior energy representative of what is going on within our internal energetic self. Meaning that whatever is happening with our four bodies (mental, emotional, spiritual, and physical) affects our chakras, which in turn are reflected in the energy field surrounding our physical body—the aura.

The auric field is a direct indication of what is going on internally. If your emotions are upset or there is confusion in your mind, it is all reflected in the aura. There are ways to protect your aura. Here are a few:

- Surround yourself with white Light from the heavens
- Smudge with sage or other herbs
- Repeat positive affirmations
- Avoid negative people
- Create a crystal grid

There are always angels and guides available to assist in any situation if it does not interfere with the Universal Law of Noninterference. Call on any one of your team members when in doubt.

Chakras take in energy from the outside world, and they also send out their own energy, represented by a frequency band, which creates the auric field. Each band vibrates at a different frequency and corresponds with a specific chakra. In this way, chakras create a bridge between the physical body and the spiritual body and act as a protective field for the physical, emotional, and mental body.

The protective field works in this way: Perhaps upon meeting someone for the first time, you felt slightly sick, had a shiver go up your arms, or just felt an aversion and didn't understand the feeling. You just felt "off." You felt there was something about the other person that made you uncomfortable. The reason was that your energy didn't match; your auric field was not on the same vibrating frequency as that of the stranger. It could have been a past life issue, or you were simply picking up energy that was uncomfortable for you.

It is usually wise to listen to what your body is telling you, whether it is when you meet another person for the first time or when you feel an aversion to a specific food or drink.

As the Starseed delves deeper and deeper into the metaphysical, more new and exciting experiences are presented by the Higher Self. The experiences are given when the Starseed is ready, and it is all a part of the unfolding of the flower.

All experiences of past and present lifetimes contribute to the soul advancement on the Path to Enlightenment. These experiences also often arouse curiosity, which then leads to more searching and more answers.

A few of these experiences include:

- A remembrance of a past life
- Visions of a past life
- Receiving a message from a deceased family member
- Seeing the spirit of a departed loved one.

*L*ove vs. Fear

During one of my group meetings in 2020, I felt guided to pose this question to the group who sat with me: What is the most prevailing, *global* vibration that is a hindrance to the ascension process and evolution? The answer was, and still is, *fear.*

Just imagine what our world would be like if that prevailing vibration was *love*! What a magnificent world this would be. If all who are reading these words were to send out that intention, that love energy, think of the difference it would make to world poverty and suffering. Intention and energy are both very powerful, so we could all make huge changes that would impact our globe in a very positive way.

John Lennon once said, "There are two basic motivating forces: fear and love. When we are afraid, we pull back from life. When we are in love, we open to all that life has to offer with passion, excitement, and acceptance. We need to learn to love ourselves first, in all our glory and our imperfections. If we cannot love ourselves, we cannot fully open to our ability to love others or our potential to create. Evolution and all hopes for a better world rest in the fearlessness and open-hearted vision of people who embrace life."

There is compelling energy in the words of John Lennon; certainly, they give us a lot to think about. Love is the most powerful force in the universe, multiverse, and omniverse—in Creation. Fear is a powerful force as well. The marvelous thing is that we get to choose which one we live by as we create our life moment by moment, choosing our actions, thoughts, words, and deeds.

We were Sourced from love, from the One who is love and light; and from that beginning, we were sent out to create our world, a world of illusion. In this illusionary world, we created fear. We are free to express either of these emotions through our God-given right of free will.

Love and fear are fundamental emotions from which many other emotions follow. One might think of them as aspects of the true emotions or results of the true emotions.

Love is followed by peace, joy, balance, forgiveness, acceptance, harmony, serenity, relaxation, and compassion.

Fear is followed by guilt, anger, jealousy, greed, judgment, sadness, pain, anxiety, stress, fatigue, and depression.

Where there is love, fear cannot survive, and where there is fear, love cannot survive; they are two polarities and cannot exist at the same time. Love is real, but fear is an illusion, an illusion that we create for ourselves. Since we have the free will to choose, our life is what we make it. We do this by creating our world through our actions and reactions. It is all about attitude!

We are used to living with the feeling of being under attack, so it has become second nature to live with stress and become defensive. This is due to cellular memory of the suffering we have experienced throughout thousands of lifetimes. We have brought into our present incarnation modern-day media reports, office competition, job insecurity, phobias, pollution, and there are many others. So, we find it difficult to believe we are free to live in love, free to relax and enjoy life, free to see the beauty around us each day.

When we finally realize the truth of this, we begin to take responsibility for our lives. We cease blaming other people and surrounding circumstances for our daily challenges, which are lessons we incarnated here to learn. When we start saying yes to love, that is what we send out to the universe, and that is what we get back. Knowing this makes our life journey a whole lot easier.

Ego — What Is It?

O f all the other challenges a Starseed faces, the ego is a huge one.

Wikipedia states that ego is a person's sense of self-esteem, self-importance, self-worth, self-respect, self-image, and self-confidence.

Ego can also be described as pride about oneself. Another definition is: the part of the mind that is responsible for reality testing and a sense of personal identity.

In ancient times, during the Atlantian and Lemurian eras, when a spirit desired to experience a lifetime on Earth, it manifested a physical body instantly, but it required constant focus to maintain the body.

So the spirit, the Higher Self, decided to create an ego, which would allow the physical body to maintain itself. Ego is the satellite, or an expansion of the soul, a part of the soul.

The soul uses the ego to take the physical body through the lifetime to gain experience and learn lessons that aid in soul growth. The ego must learn enough to lift its vibration to its higher spiritual nature. When it has gained enough experience and learned the lessons set forth, it can then merge with the Higher Self and ascend.

Now, having said all this, how does our ego affect us in our day-to-day living? Are we able to control our ego? And, if so, how do we do this?

First, know that the ego is necessary to our existence. It is who we are. We need our ego to get around in this third-dimensional planet we find ourselves on because it is a planet of duality and challenges. In order to further understand the ego, we need to realize that the job of the ego is to defend and protect "self."

During primitive times, the ego operated in the fight-or-flight mode, which was our way to survive. Since we are no longer living as primitive beings, having evolved and become more consciously aware, we no longer need that part of the ego, but the ego has not learned that. This means that we must be more aware of our ego-self.

When I first began to meditate, the biggest difficulty I encountered were thoughts that caused disruption to my meditation process, such as ones of mundane tasks. *What shall I cook tomorrow? I need to make a grocery list. The laundry needs to be done.*

My guardian angel told me to quiet my mind by enclosing my thoughts in a bubble and setting it aside until I was finished meditating. She told me the reason my mind was so busy during meditation was that my ego was afraid I would "go someplace" and not return.

The ego needed control, due to its fear. "Aha!" you say, there is the fear rearing its head again. Yes, it was. I eventually realized that the way to put aside the fear was through conscious breathing, by focusing on breath. Conscious breathing is simply focusing on each inhale and exhale. Also, it is a very effective method to calm the ego during any meditation.

The ego can be a mischief maker, causing all sorts of problems by controlling our life if we do not maintain conscious awareness at all times. Ego is very adept at justifying—me being right and you wrong, being a complainer, showing and feeling resentment. This is all done to protect "self." Our role is to recognize this and then calm and manage the ego.

The ego likes control and power; however, too much control and power can obstruct our channel to Spirit by getting in the way of the flow of grace. This is a huge hindrance to achieving communication with Spirit and one we must overcome to attain soul growth in this incarnation.

Here are a few ways to manage the ego:

- Think before you speak—control your words.
- Silence is golden—it is better to be silent than to be right.

- Focus on your potential, not your perceived limitations. When you are comfortable in your own skin and love yourself, the need for comparison disappears.
- See the divinity in others and recognize that all are God's children.

$\mathcal{U}$*nconditional Love*

My spiritual path has been ongoing for many years, and at one time, I pondered the true meaning of *unconditional love*. After much thought and meditation, I finally understood the concept.

Unconditional love seems to indicate that we as Seekers must love everyone and everything unconditionally. And we should—but not in the way we might think. It simply means that we must accept another's journey, no matter what they do or say. It does not mean that we must like it or even understand it, but we need to unconditionally accept where another soul is on their chosen path without any vestige of judgment. If our energies do not match or no longer match, we are free to send a person love and then bow out and continue our separate ways.

A dedicated and determined Starseed begins to learn how to accept others who do not, will not, or cannot understand them, even though situations may arise that are problematic. It is all about the varying levels of consciousness that exist within our society.

Acceptance of others is in direct correlation to the level of consciousness that a disciple is operating in. As the consciousness rises, so does the ability to deal with difficult or negative people or situations in a loving, compassionate, and nonjudgmental way.

A wise young lady once said to me, "What other people think of me is none of my business. That is their world." Our task is to pay attention to our own thoughts, words, and deeds and then allow another to walk their path the way they choose. When I learned this truth, it was incredibly freeing for me. I felt like a weight had been lifted, and it was.

Another element of unconditional love is when we apply it to ourselves. It is much easier to accept, forgive, and not judge another than it is to love, forgive, and not judge ourselves. If we cannot love and accept ourselves, we cannot truly love and accept another. It is just that simple.

Self-Love, Self-Forgiveness, Nonjudgment of Self

As we travel along the road to enlightenment, some of the most challenging issues we face are learning to love and forgive ourselves. Self-love is crucial to soul evolvement. It seems simple enough, but it is one of the most difficult things for an aspiring Starseed to do. In order to love ourselves, we first must learn forgiveness of self and avoid self-judgment.

It's often easy to forgive others but not ourselves because we don't love ourselves enough. Lack of self-forgiveness stems from self-judgment, which leads to the inability to love our own self. Judgment of self is a hindrance to advancing in consciousness.

We as aspiring disciples will often judge ourselves harshly, and that puts us in the lower vibrations. When we judge ourselves for making a mistake, we feel guilt and shame. Guilt and shame, along with fear, are huge burdens we place on ourselves.

We have incarnated on planet Earth many times, and through that, we have acquired beliefs that have followed us through incarnation after incarnation. It is *this* incarnation where we chose to drop those old beliefs that are inhibiting our soul progression. It is important to remember that we are not perfect; we are wearing human form, living in a dense environment fraught with challenging situations every day.

Speaking or thinking negatively about ourselves or comparing ourselves to others and, in that comparison, coming up short, is self-limiting. We need to focus on our potential, not our limitations. We need to realize that every experience has value and then come to a place where we are satisfied with who and what we are. So, it is important that we are kind to ourselves. We do make mistakes, but perhaps we can turn that "mistake" into an opportunity by learning from it.

Mistake or Opportunity

Adversity can be our best friend because we learn through adversity. Contained within our soul contracts are certain lessons we choose to learn. When there is an issue in our life that is blocking our forward momentum, our Higher Self will place situations in front of us repeatedly until we get it right, until we overcome that obstacle so that we are able to move on and open the next door.

Through experience, we gain knowledge and understanding and are then able to reach our highest potential. This awareness provides the power to take control of our lives and create our reality moment by moment.

Wise is the soul who learns from a perceived "mistake." Instead of beating ourselves up about something we said or did that we later regret, it's better to mentally take a step back from the situation and try to look at it objectively.

Our human side will surface occasionally, and that is normal. We are all here to learn and attain soul growth. We stumble, sometimes fall, pick ourselves up, and move ever forward. However, we *are* responsible for our thoughts, words, and actions. Blaming someone else does not help us learn; it is an easy way out. Taking responsibility for what we think, say, and do shows soul maturity.

A good way to make the most of a negative situation is to realize that it's not the situation that holds the importance; it is what we do with it. Do we act or react?

Which is more important—to participate in negativity or move on and gain soul growth from this drama we call *life*?

Expectations

Expectations are defined as believing that something is going to happen a certain way or believing that something should happen a certain way.

Anticipation is a strong belief that you will get something you want.

Seek to prevent disappointment by establishing in advance what can realistically be achieved or delivered by a person or a course of action.

An expectation, which is a belief that is centered on the future, may or may not be realistic. Then, a result that we deem as less than advantageous gives rise to disappointment.

Expectations are a part of everyday life. We all have expectations, meaning we all set ourselves up for disappointment, especially regarding what another person will do or say. The best way to avoid disappointment is to accept others the way they are and not expect more than they are willing to give.

When we expect too much from another and they don't live up to those expectations, we experience disappointment, which most often leads to placing blame on that person. It is wise to remember that no one can hurt our feelings or cause sadness or disappointment unless we allow it. We all have the power to control how we think and feel. We have power over our own emotions.

Once we accept this truth, life becomes easier because we put the responsibility on ourselves, where it belongs.

There is a saying: We can only control what we think, say, or do; we have no control over what others say, think, or do. This is true. However, we can control our *reactions* to whatever situation we face.

Peace begins when expectation ends.

~ Sri Chinmoy
(August 27, 1931–October 11, 2007)

Mysticism, Healing, and Energy

A long the highway to enlightenment, a dedicated Starseed will often dive deep into the world of mysticism with great enthusiasm. In their pursuit for more knowledge, they will learn about various classes, groups, meetings, and workshops that are offered in their area and then explore each one that piques their interest.

They will be drawn to whatever is most needed on their journey at that time, then move on to another when they are ready for it. For some, it is a never-ending quest, as one bit of knowledge leads to the desire for more. Every door must be opened, each topic explored and digested as the information and energy are mulled over and processed.

One teacher, one workshop, one psychic will lead to another, and more and more will be presented to the Starseed for investigation as they move forward along their path. The world of energy surfaces for exploration. Healing techniques such as Reiki, tapping, and massage may draw the interest of a disciple, along with yoga and tai chi.

There are various forms of yoga and tai chi, and all are beneficial to the body. These are ancient, gentle methods of healing the body and soul, and they are also very effective ways to raise the vibration of a Seeker. Both yoga and tai chi can be a practice of meditation.

The Seeker will learn of the power and energy of crystals, astrology, the study of the astral, numerology and the mystery of numbers, maybe even the deep world of the shamans. There are a variety of avenues to explore, and the dedicated Seeker will never get their fill, never be sated. Disciples will search for and find shops full of crystals, essential oils, fascinating books, statues, collectibles, and unique jewelry to purchase or just look at. The mystical aromas that are present and the energy contained within those dwellings are akin to soul food. The desire for more learning and more experiences expands with each morsel of information, until there is no door left unopened and no stone left unturned.

There is magic everywhere—in nature, in the pebbles, flora, and fauna. Then comes the knowledge of the world of elementals, divas, sprites, and faeries. They do exist, they are real, but most of us just cannot see them. When that truth is accepted by the aspirant, more magic happens. One sees the beauty in everything—in nature, in the animal, plant, and mineral kingdoms.

Each area that is explored brings the Seeker closer and closer to Spirit, to their Higher Self, to their team of angels and guides, to Source energy, to the wondrous world of the Great Unknown. Then their quest may turn to the sphere of densities and dimensions. This fascinating subject is explored and explained in more detail later in this book.

Along with the pursuit for more knowledge comes a rise in consciousness. With each avenue of searching, with each new development, the aspirant expands their consciousness.

$\mathscr{C}$rystals

$\mathbf{M}$any Starseeds discover and then focus on the delightful world of crystals. Crystals are a part of the first dimension, and they do have a consciousness. Each crystal contains its own form of energy and therefore has specific vibrations. Their uses are numerous, complex, and powerful.

Crystals are used mainly for healing the mind and body on Earth at this time. They are used in the higher realms, and always have been, for most aspects of energy work. The healing properties of crystals were known and utilized in the ancient world.

There were several early civilizations that inhabited the earth—such as the Atlanteans, Lemurians, Mayans, and Aztecs—and these advanced, ancient civilizations knew the value and power of crystals and used them for amplifying the power of most anything: agriculture, technology, spiritual growth, transportation, and, of course, healing. Crystals were also used to enhance their rituals.

All of that was lost here on Earth over time, and knowledge of the power of crystals has been kept hidden from most of society in modern times. That is changing now, and perhaps soon the power of crystals will once again be front and center in our world for all the population.

When you feel the desire to delve into the magical world of crystals, such as taking a workshop for more knowledge about them or purchasing a few, use your intuition. Choose the ones you are drawn to. Since crystals have a consciousness, they will "speak" to you, and if you "listen," they will tell you which ones you need. It's all about following your intuition.

$\mathcal{W}$orking with Energy

E verything in Creation is energy. Energy cannot be created nor destroyed but can be changed, moved, or transformed, and it exists in numerous forms. As the Seeker traverses the varied and sometimes complex path through life, many are drawn to the ancient healing arts such as qigong, tai chi, massage, and Reiki.

We use energy in our everyday lives without even realizing it most of the time. Our thoughts are energy. When we think the same thing over and over, that thought becomes denser each time, and eventually it manifests into matter. That is how powerful we really are. The importance of our thoughts is of such magnitude that we create our reality, and often this concept escapes our conscious mind.

We have the ability and the power to shape both our inner and outer world just through our thoughts. When we combine that knowledge with intention, we are limitless in our creativity! Using intention magnifies our thoughts so that whatever we are focusing on assumes more power. And thus, we can create miracles. Meditation is a good example, especially group meditation, when many people place their focus on one thought.

What is little known or often forgotten is that when we use the vibration of love plus intention and focus, we then energetically call in the world of Spirit.

Whatever we focus on with loving intent is magnified ten-, a hundred-, a thousand-fold, or even more by Spirit! We can ask them to join us in our focus or just know that they will be with us.

We are often told by Spirit to monitor our thoughts, to be aware of our thoughts, because of the power we unknowingly hold. Thoughts can work the opposite way as well. When we focus on negativity, that is what we create.

Living in the density of this world can be very difficult, and many souls live in fear, guilt, shame, anger, anxiety. When this negative energy goes out into the ethers, that is what we receive in return. It's called the Law of Attraction. This is one way in which we as humanity contribute to the density we exist in.

Learning about Vibrational Frequency

This subject fits right in with Energy. While navigating the road to enlightenment, one is told to "keep your vibration high." That can be puzzling to a new Seeker. We all aspire to learn, and there can be so many new terms and phrases to explore. What does vibration have to do with frequency? How does it all affect the disciple?

Raising our vibration is essential to soul growth. Our bodies are made up of molecules. Frequency is the rate at which molecules vibrate. The molecules of our body oscillate back and forth at a certain frequency. The measure of the speed of this frequency is known as vibrational frequency. The greater the speed of the vibrating molecules, the higher our vibration is and the more Light we are able to hold. In this way, we increase our level of consciousness.

When our consciousness rises, we take in more information, convert it to knowledge, and then we are able to grasp more complicated concepts. It is occasionally referred to as "seeing the bigger picture" or "thinking outside the box."

When we keep our bodies vibrating at a high enough frequency, we can more easily move along our path, more easily evolve, more easily learn the lessons we are faced with on this journey of ours. When our body's vibratory frequency is low, we feel sluggish, irritable, out of sorts, and nothing seems to go right for us. Therefore, doing what we can to keep a high vibration is imperative to happiness, soul growth, and our evolution.

Here are some of the many ways to raise our vibration:

Clear and balance the chakras.

A few of these methods were covered in a previous section.

Show, speak, or jot down gratitude.

We have so much to be grateful for, and verbalizing or writing this down makes us think about what these things are, thus, making us feel grateful.

Chant "OM" three times or more.

The continued recitation of OM fills one with peace, calmness, tranquility, and serenity. When we recite OM, it brings us closer to our true nature, our own pure self. OM is the spirit of God, the vibration of Creation.

Meditate.

This is one of the most powerful ways to raise your vibration. Meditation quiets the mind, body, and emotions and allows communication to flow from Spirit.

Monitor your thoughts.

This is so very important! When we have positive thoughts, our vibratory frequency stays high, and when we send out negativity to the universe, that is what we get back. Focus on what you want, not what you don't want.

Go out and connect with nature.

Walk barefoot on the earth if the temperature allows. Appreciate the beauty around you. Just connect. Hold the intention on your inhale to breathe in the vibration of peace. Using your intention on the exhale, breathe out any negative energy.

Avoid mainstream media.

Avoid the news, avoid the violence, avoid the advertising. The mainstream media generates fear and negativity, and it is under the control of the dark forces. They deliver to us as "news" exactly what they want us to hear and see, which is not always for our highest and best good.

Heal and let go of the past.

Forgive yourself and others. Learn from the past; then let it go and move on.

Declutter your home and workplace.

Clutter causes your energy to become scattered; it can cause irritability and loss of concentration.

Surround yourself with positive people.

Positive people raise you up. Negative people pull you down.

Share a hug.

Hugging increases bonding, relaxes the body, relieves pain, increases empathy and understanding, relieves depression, elevates one's mood, balances the nervous system, alleviates stress, improves heart health, and decreases the heart rate.

Eat healthy foods.

Avoid junk food and alcohol.

Laugh.

Find humor in a situation. Learn to laugh at yourself and to be kind to yourself.

<u>Exercise.</u>

Exercise releases endorphins, which trigger a positive feeling in the body. Endorphins also interact with the receptors in the brain that reduce your perception of pain.

Gratitude

Although feeling and expressing gratitude is a significant part of moving along the path to enlightenment, its importance is often diminished. Gratitude affects the energetic body by raising one's vibration and works in amazing ways with the Law of Attraction, for what you feel and project out is what will come back to you energetically. Also, when you're in a grateful mood, grateful emotions are more likely to flow.

Gratitude is a form of prayer, a way of saying thank you. Instead of praying for something you want, give thanks for what you already have. No matter how bad circumstances may be, there is always something to be grateful for. It's important to remember that when life seems difficult, you can see the difficulties as lessons that give wisdom and then be grateful for the lesson and the wisdom.

If you are in a slump, feeling sad or lonely, one way to raise your vibration is to make a list of all the things in your life you have, to be grateful for. You may surprise yourself! When finished with the list, you will no doubt have changed your mindset.

Gratitude is the music of the heart when its chords are swept by the breeze of kindness.

~ Author Unknown

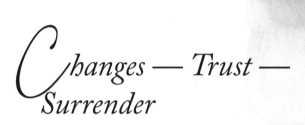

Changes — Trust — Surrender

There are phases during our journey when we encounter chaotic, challenging situations as we dig ourselves out of the mire that we have been experiencing for centuries. It can often be a time of massive change, of releasing old beliefs and patterns—a time for cleansing. It is a huge conflict between the old and the new.

Sometimes, it seems we are not making any progress in our work of lifting ourselves and others, but that is an illusion. We are constantly raising our level of consciousness and that of the collective as we move ever forward toward our goal of mass ascension.

We recognize the challenge, deal with it, and then process the changes we have brought about. It is not an easy task, and the battle is an inner one, an emotional one.

Silent but intense. Outwardly, it appears that nothing is going on, but inwardly there is a lot happening.

Processing the changes takes time, sometimes days, weeks, months, or even years, depending on the severity of the change. Many do not realize what is happening to them, to their lives, to their days and nights. Much occurs in the night, in our sleep time, that we are not consciously aware of. This may manifest as physical discomfort, such as loss of appetite, headaches, an upset stomach, or perhaps joint problems.

Change also affects our mental body. We might wake confused, not completely back in our body and wondering what just occurred, or we may feel a huge sense of sadness or despair for no apparent reason. We may wake too soon and hear ourselves talking to some unknown, unseen being, and we may feel exhausted and not know why. There are so many ways our four bodies are affected by our sleep time activities. Being aware of this is a big help.

Our inner bodies are being changed. Our DNA and our cells are changing from carbon-based to crystalline as we take in more Light, and it takes patience, perseverance, and the ability to love ourselves, to not judge ourselves when feelings and memories arise that make us uncomfortable. There is also emotional discomfort as we face past lives and memories.

As we release old patterns and belief systems, as we purge ourselves of everything that is keeping us in the lower frequencies and vibrations, things may seem chaotic and painful. This is a necessary purge, because the more we release the old, the more Light we are able to take in and hold, and, as this occurs, we begin to move up into a higher state of awareness.

Before we assumed the mantle of human form, we chose our path. Then we were made to forget all that we knew, and we stumble through earthly life sometimes thinking, *This is just too difficult!* We have the free will to choose any timeline we wish to, but that doesn't always allow us to move forward. If there is a lesson that we need to learn, then our Higher Self will place that situation before us again and again until we finally catch on and make the choice to stay on the path.

When and if we stop resisting Spirit, our life smooths out and begins to flow with ease. When our vibration matches that of the universe, peace is the result.

Eventually, if we are a serious Seeker, we surrender to our Higher Power, we surrender all that does not serve us well and remember that we are not a victim. We are divine Beings having a human experience.

We are here to learn, here to work in service to others, here to help lift the planet and humanity by living in love, feeling compassion for our fellow humans, and knowing that we are ever loved and supported by a multitude of heavenly Beings, our galactic family, and our angelic team who work with us always. We are never alone.

The Shadow People

Come out, come out, wherever you are. Why are you hiding in the shadows? Come out and shine your bright and beautiful Light. You cannot grow in the shadows. You need the Light. The Light is there for you to evolve. The Light is warm, loving, and everlasting. The Light is eternity, yours for the taking. Will you not avail yourself of this wonderful gift—the gift of life, love, peace, and harmony?

So many beautiful souls hide in the shadows. They feel there is something more to life, they feel dissatisfied and restless, but they continue to stay in the shadowland because of fear. They are afraid to acknowledge their divinity, afraid to come out into the open and let the world see and know who they really are.

The fear is from ego—fear of ridicule from their friends, family, acquaintances, the neighbors, or anyone else who is not on the spiritual path. What these souls do not understand is that the "friends" are not really friends if they sit in judgment and do not respect another's choice, another's way of life.

It can be difficult to cope with family members who do not agree with the spiritual path, especially if they follow a particular religion. One way to face this challenge is to ask that they respect your choice even if they do not agree with it.

Acquaintances are just that: they come and go in your life, and usually their opinion does not make a huge impact. The same can be said for neighbors.

Some souls begin to follow the path of a Seeker, then get caught up in everyday life—perhaps a new relationship, a new job placement, or the loss of a job, maybe even the death of a loved one—and all these circumstances can affect life in a significant way and impact the spiritual focus of the Seeker.

Sometimes, a spiritual experience will prompt a soul to come out of the shadowland into the Light, and then a change in life happens and that soul goes back into hiding for a brief time or maybe for the rest of the incarnation.

Occasionally, a soul will begin to experience the stirrings of awakening and not realize what is happening. The body will often "step in" and manifest physical discomfort as a way of saying, "Move forward on your path." This stirring can come in different forms and affect different parts of the body. There are times when the third-dimensional consciousness resists and refuses to accept the urging of the Higher Self. That is a choice each incarnated soul has, called free will.

Be brave, dear souls, follow the urgings of Spirit. Come out of the shadows and shine your beautiful Light for all to see. It will be worth it!

The Matrix

In the spiritual community, souls who are awakening often speak of the "matrix." The matrix is an energetic grid that surrounds our planet outside of its auric field, about fifteen miles (twenty-four kilometers) above the earth.

Eons ago, in our galaxy, horrific, catastrophic wars were common. The wars were known as the Great Galactic Wars and continued for millions of years. These wars caused the death and destruction of planets, and many lives were lost. The ancient civilizations that participated in this warfare possessed starships that were the size of small planets or moons, and their technology was highly developed. During one of these conflicts, two great starships destroyed each other through nuclear warfare.

They bombarded each other with their weapons of death, each sustaining mortal damage. As the ships careened wildly through our solar system in their death throes, a gigantic chunk from one of the ships plummeted toward Terah (Earth, an anagram of Terah), crashing into her. Major trauma to her great body resulted, and she lurched, tilted on her axis, and was in danger of being knocked off her orbit and veering out into space.

Witness to this carnage was Mother God, the Angelic Kingdom, and countless galactics. Under the direction of Mother God, the Angelic Kingdom took control. They placed a field of healing, stabilizing energy around Terah. This energetic grid later became known as the matrix.

Approximately a billion years ago, Terah came under the domination of a group of dark forces; they were malevolent, greedy, power-hungry extraterrestrials who inhabited various planets in the galaxy. They renamed Terah "Earth," then corrupted the inhabitants through abuse, terror, and injustice. The dark ones are still here, although their power is vastly diminished.

Earth was not to be left in peace. More destruction to her great body was on the horizon. Long ago, during the Atlantean and Lemurian era, Atlantis was taken over by the dark ones, who created animosity between Atlantis and Lemuria. More warring began. The result of these wars was almost total annihilation of both landmasses. Hawaii, Fiji, and New Zealand are remnants of the Lemurian continent. Atlantis completely sank beneath the waves.

Through the dark ones' ruthless control of Earth, humanity fell from a fifth-dimensional civilization to a third. When this happened, Gaia, the consciousness of the planet, chose to drop with the inhabitants by taking human, physical form. Archangel Gaia has incarnated multiple times throughout the ages, assisting humanity to raise their vibration and attain mass ascension. That is where we are now as a civilization.

The fall from fifth-dimensional to three-dimensional was a direct result of the various mechanisms used to control humanity, some of which were wars (population control), religion (fear, guilt, and suppression of a huge part of the population), chemicals in our air, food, and water, and many more.

Humanity has suffered injustice and abuse for millions of years, and this has been, and is, expressed in thoughts, words, deeds, and emotions. The negative energy from the masses has gone out into the atmosphere and settled in the energy field around the planet, causing it to transform from healing energy to negative energy.

Souls decide to incarnate here on Earth with good intentions: to live a loving, compassionate life, learn lessons, and evolve. However, once here, having taken the Veil of Forgetfulness, that journey becomes much more difficult, and many lose their way. They lose sight of the Light, stray to the dark side, and become lost. Their good intentions are lost as well.

Due to the abusive influence of the dark forces, many humans become impoverished, homeless, drug-and alcohol-addicted, reverting to inhumane treatment of each other and sending their thoughts of despair, sadness, hopelessness, and anguish out into the ethers, which settles in the energy field that surrounds the earth, intensifying the negativity year after year.

This creates a prison of sorts that keeps souls coming back repeatedly to learn, grow, evolve, and shed their Light. Each time that a soul incarnates on planet Earth, they wish to choose love, and some do exactly that; others fall to the energies of power, greed, and corruption and very often cannot complete their life journey as planned.

Once a physical body is released and the soul returns home to their galactic family and friends, they are aware of not fulfilling their contract. Various lessons were not learned, and certain karma was not completed. The soul then incarnates once again to accomplish their goals. When this takes place again and again, it becomes what is known as the "karmic wheel."

There is good news. Through the awakening of much of humanity in the past decade or so, the Light on this planet has increased to a level that allows the galactics to intervene and assist. The dark ones are in disarray and running scared. They still do create some degree of havoc but are neutralized in many ways.

The matrix is gradually disintegrating and being replaced with healing energy once again by the Light forces. This transition is a smooth, gradual process that occurs as humanity continues to reach for Spirit and raise their vibration. Soon this planet will be free to pursue her destiny, and humanity will continue to pursue their destiny, which is spiritual enlightenment!

Truth and Discernment

During my years of exploring the world of spirituality and all the facets of that journey, I have realized that there are various versions of "the truth." Along with those versions comes the need for discernment.

An aspiring soul on a dedicated road to enlightenment will be told, or read, or watch an online video about a particular subject, and then it is the responsibility of the aspirant to use discernment in what has been read, heard, or watched. It can be a challenging task, but it is necessary in order to find the truth.

We are all truth Seekers who desire more knowledge, and that path can be filled with hindrances. Using our intuition, listening to our "inner voice," is the best way to separate fact from fiction, truth from fabrication. In that way, we come from the heart, not the mind. The key is to allow the heart to rule.

Throughout my years of working with the public, I have listened to numerous people describe their experiences, and I have learned that there are many ways to hear, see, and integrate information that is given to us. Since we are all different, our methods of processing this information differ.

We, as Lightworkers, are all heading the same way, but like the branches of a tree, we grow in various directions. I have noticed that we can each be given similar dreams, visions, or messages but then we may arrive at varying conclusions.

Sometimes this information pertains to the future; it is not intended to inform us that it will happen today or tomorrow. In the higher dimensions, there is no time. While inhabiting this planet, we operate on linear time, but that is not so in the higher realms.

The messages that arrive as visions can be in the form of symbols. Symbols are a tool used by Spirit to make us aware of a situation, therefore, we cannot always interpret the messages literally.

It is important to always respect another soul's opinion even if it conflicts with our own. We need to come from a place of nonjudgment regarding others' belief systems and the ways they process information.

Lord Sananda (Jesus) gave me a brief message one day that I use in my own work, and that is: "Choose love." If we make a habit of choosing love in any situation, judgment and disrespect cannot exist.

The Pathway to Stardom

The pathway to Stardom is through the heart.

We as incarnated souls are all on a journey—an exciting, challenging, ever-changing path of life. Our journeys are diverse, and we experience multiple emotions as we navigate the various experiences that we planned preincarnate.

During the creation of our special drama, we are aware of our obligation to take the Veil of Forgetfulness, meaning that in order to complete our plan, we are not permitted to remember our life in the stars. If we did remember, our yearning to go home would be detrimental to our learning and growth.

Many souls are eager to experience an incarnation on this planet because it is a difficult place to live; the lessons and situations are often demanding and complicated, which can be a blessing in disguise by giving incarnates the opportunity to make a giant leap forward in evolution.

We do have the perfect champion to support us throughout our journey, and that champion is our Higher Self, the part of us that stayed back, the part of us that still exists in the stars. This being, the greater part of ourselves, is our guide through this life. She/he is ever patient, ever tolerant, never judges, and is always willing to assist us in any way permitted that does not interfere with our free will.

To further explain who this great being is, I wish to write from a personal point of view. I have a delightful connection with my Higher Self. The connection is a gift that I have given to myself every moment since I came into awareness of this Being, and it was not easily accomplished. It was a learning process and took years of inner work for me to trust my Higher Power and surrender completely. She was a force within me that unceasingly urged me forward, with a nudge here or there and, occasionally, a huge shove that I could not ignore.

To acquire this gift, one has only to be willing and allow the greater part of yourself into your heart. Trust is paramount—trust that your divine self knows what is best for you, he/she oversees your journey, and everything that happens along the way is directed with love and precision.

When that heart connection is made, magic happens! Your life flows more smoothly, and you reach a level of understanding, knowing that love is the greatest force in creation. You follow your guidance and begin to trust your own intuition with more confidence.

When you are willing to create that bridge between two worlds, the spiritual and the physical, you open a doorway to the higher dimensions, a doorway to the stars, to home. Your home is in the stars! You are not from here; you are from the stars, you are a galactic being, a star being, and your heart connection with your divine self is your way home.

When a disciple merges their consciousness with that of their divine self, they have "touched the face of God." The love that is present in this merging and connecting is truly out of this world!

Attaining Self-Mastery

Souls volunteer to have a lifetime on this planet with joyous anticipation; then, occasionally, a small number will lose their way, forgetting about the Divine and the Light. What happens to them? Why do they stray from their plan?

It's easy to choose love in situations when everything is going well, but it's a lot more difficult when pain and suffering are present. When people are hungry, homeless, abused, sick, or impoverished, their focus is not on their connection to Spirit, unless it's to ask God to save them from their hardship. In some instances, they may even deny God. "There's no God. Why is this happening to me? God, why are you doing this to me?" God is often blamed for suffering, and this is a useless waste of energy; God gave each soul the gift of free will, and what we do with that free will is up to us.

We are the ones in charge of our life path. Our Higher Self is our main guide and the director of the plan, but once we take human form, as a free soul, we have the choice of free will, the choice to decide what we want to do while in human form. We create our own reality (life) moment by moment, and we generate our own dramas using free will by making each decision throughout our day. We alone are responsible for our life choices.

It's easier to chide or attack another for our own misery than admit to ourselves that *we* are the one who made the choice. And, after doing so, we often complain about it. Self-responsibility is once again put on hold, and the onus is placed on someone else.

Many large organizations take advantage of people because they can. They can because we allow it. Consider the big banks and their credit card charges. Countless individuals purchase things because they want them, not always because they need them. It's very easy to purchase an item when there is no cash involved and worry about paying for it later. When "later" arrives, it can cause a lot of stress, anxiety, and family disagreements.

There are times when credit is required, but often, it is overindulgence. Our overindulgence gives the banks the right to charge whatever they wish.

Pain and suffering can sometimes be caused by our own weaknesses, such as addictions to drugs, alcohol, and overeating, which can then lead to ill-health, family separation, despair, and hopelessness. Again, it is due to lack of personal power and restraint.

We as humans enjoy our comfort zone and sometimes close our eyes to what is really happening on this planet simply because it can be very disturbing. We don't wish to see it or believe it, so we shut it out. Facing the truth about the injustice and abuse that is prevalent in our communities and the world can be unpleasant, so it's much easier to ignore the plight of others than do something about it. By ignoring it, we allow it.

Then there is the issue of "acceptance of others" and how we sometimes view others as different in our diverse population.

When we judge others by what they wear, how they speak, or the cultural disparities that are evident, we create separation. Our unwillingness to accept others corrupts our connection to Spirit through the emotions of anger, fear, distrust, and, in some situations, hatred and the desire for vengeance. For some, it's less bothersome to blame others for being different (as we see it) and for not accepting the differences than it is to take responsibility and admit the truth of our own bias.

In many instances, humanity refuses to accept responsibility by blaming the government, the banks, the medical community, the teachers, the police, their neighbors—anyone but themselves. It truly is time that we as a collective take responsibility for our own lives.

We came to this planet voluntarily; no one forced us. We formulated our own life plan, and we decided what lessons we wanted to learn, and which karma needed to be cleared. Occasionally, we plan a challenging journey for ourselves, and while experiencing those challenges, we play the victim and often blame others for our woes. When we understand and admit this, we begin to mature emotionally and spiritually.

Exactly what does "taking responsibility" mean? Does it mean being strong instead of weak? What is weakness? Is our weakness allowing ego to take control of life? Ego wants control. Ego is hurt feelings, self-pity, anger, frustration. Strength is managing the ego, assuming responsibility for our own self. The act of being able to manage the ego is self-mastery, mastery of self.

I and only I am in charge of
and responsible for my
thoughts, words, deeds, and emotions.
No one else.
It is called self-mastery.

The Secret to Life

The secret to life is a mystery that has been reflected on for centuries by the ancients and by those of us in the world of today. Why are we here? Where did we come from? What are souls?

Existence is a cycle; a cycle of birth, life, and death.

Some people believe that we just "happen" through the merging of an egg and sperm, and presto, a body is formed and born into the world. That is partially true, but then what about the soul? Where does it come from and what is it?

The chemical components that make up a body can be built from many sources, but only God can create souls. Souls are light, love, and consciousness. The consciousness is the God spark within us.

We all began from Source energy, the One of all that is. Source is pure energy, an equal balance of masculine and feminine energy, one great consciousness. It is not a physical form. So how does this Prime Creator experience all that is available in Its own magnificent Creation?

It subdivides Itself into billions and billions of fragments called souls (consciousness), then sends those parts of Itself out to experience life in all forms, in all realities.

Those fragments are the sparks of divinity that reside within each and every one of us. We are all part of the greater whole, all part of the Prime Creator, and that is where the saying "we are all one" comes from. We truly are all one. Everything that each soul experiences during a lifetime—all the situations, happy or otherwise—go back to Source, and this is how the Supreme Consciousness experiences physical reality.

A soul is cast, given the gift of free will, and then sent out to explore various realities. Each soul has a distinct journey, a particular drama to explore, different lessons to learn, and karma to take care of. They plan situations that include other souls and choose parents, family, mates, and lifestyles. There are souls who came in for the express purpose of ascension, and there are others who choose not to ascend but to just experience life at this time in the amazing history of this beautiful planet.

It's all a mask behind a veil, in which innumerable states of mind reside.

The mask is what hides the reality. What we live is an illusion because we plan our life drama, then take human form. We are actresses and actors playing out the plan that we formulated preincarnate. The director of our great plan is our Higher Self, the part of us that stayed back to love, guide, and support us through the lifetime.

The veil is the Veil of Forgetfulness that we are all required to assume when we come here. It is necessary in order to advance in evolution. When we take on the mantle of human form, the opportunity for rapid spiritual advancement is great. Earth is sometimes referred to as "the school of hard knocks." It is a difficult place to live because of the oppression humanity has endured for millions of years.

The oppression is due to the patriarchal society that was established on this planet about a billion years ago by an off-planet species for the purposes of power and greed. That is not entirely a bad thing for us; it can be an opportunity to overcome fear, guilt, shame, and other low vibrations by reaching for Spirit with love, thus offering all of us the chance to take a leap forward in evolution.

Lastly, the "innumerable states of mind" often means our ego. Throughout our life, we hold many different states of mind, such as joy, love, peace, hope, compassion, fear, doubt, greed, guilt, shame, anger, resentment, and jealousy. Learning to manage the ego is a huge part of life; it is vital to soul advancement.

When we are in the lower vibrations, it is difficult, if not impossible, to connect to Spirit, because that connection requires love, and love comes from the heart.

Negative emotions and love cannot occupy the same space at the same time; it is impossible.

The "innumerable states of mind" can also mean a choice of which timeline we wish to pursue. A timeline is a pathway you choose to follow; it is wherever we place our awareness. We all have been given the gift of free will so we can choose any path that presents itself. In so doing, we then must take responsibility for that choice.

Source energy is love, we are love, and when we choose to take physical form, we choose from the vibration of love. Our love for humanity, the planet, and ourselves originates from the desire to evolve as we navigate the adventurous road back to Source. The Veil of Forgetfulness teaches us valuable lessons in life. It's as if we actually do wear a mask and a veil, and the true origins of our life in the stars are forgotten.

Our chosen journey can be fraught with challenges that sometimes seem insurmountable. We see others as different—different skin colors, different beliefs, different traditions—and from that, we form judgments about them and the way they live.

Life's burdens may cause us to stray from the vibration of love and choose anger at another. That is when we need to forgive ourselves. Sometimes, we make choices that we are sorry for and then find it difficult to forgive and love ourselves. Some of the most important lessons we learn are self-love, self-forgiveness, and nonjudgment of self. Expand that to love, forgiveness, and nonjudgment of others.

When we remember that we created our human dramas, when we stop blaming others for our woes and begin to take responsibility for our life, that is when we begin to raise our vibration and our consciousness. Raising our consciousness enables us to go one step further and choose unconditional love for others. This simply means accepting another's journey by accepting the path and choices of another. The acceptance comes from understanding that each soul plans their own life path.

Expanded consciousness helps us understand the bigger picture, to think outside of ourselves, to realize that balance is needed in all things. There is no judgment in the higher realms; everything just is. There is no right or wrong. Judgment is a human trait that we inflict upon ourselves, for we are all mirror images of each other.

The goal is to choose love in all things. Love is the answer in every situation. The secret to life is love.

What Happens When We Die

What happens when our physical body dies? This question has been discussed throughout our history by many people, and there are a variety of different versions of that occurrence. When humanity does not have access to the truth, or through acquired beliefs has a false impression of why we are here and where we come from, the imagination takes over and fabricates an answer. It is also so with the process of transitioning from this world to our true home.

While in the higher dimensions, before we take human form, we prepare our life plan, and contained within that plan are all the situations and lessons that we would like to experience while in the physical body, which includes the details around our birth and our physical death.

There are no accidents or mistakes; the life plan is guided precisely by the Higher Self.

The only deviation is when we use our free will and leave prematurely through suicide. Even then, there is no judgment from the higher dimensions. It is just a matter of coming back to replay the drama, and that is only if we choose to on a soul level. Our souls are eternal; there is no hurry to be anywhere or do anything. We have eternity to complete any incarnation we desire.

Birth, life, and death are processes, a series of experiences and situations. We are all here to evolve in whichever way we choose, and we have the gift of free will to make any choice we wish to throughout our lives. Because of the choices a soul makes, it may find itself caught up in negative energy patterns that create hurdles the soul may not be able to overcome, making it more difficult to advance in evolution.

Each soul's afterlife may be different from another's. There are many levels of consciousness/awareness that a soul occupies during a lifetime. When the physical body dies, the soul goes to the afterlife level that it has reached during the incarnation and thus experiences that afterlife.

One type of afterlife is the fourth dimension, known as nirvana. If the soul's vibration at the death of the physical body is at that level, then that is the afterlife the soul will experience.

Nirvana is the dimension where a soul can attend healing and learning temples, and in that way, it can raise its vibration to the level of the fifth dimension, which is necessary to exist in the higher realms. No soul is ever left behind. Our Higher Self is always there for us, and when the time is right, the soul will return home.

When the adventure is over, when lessons are learned, karma is dealt with, or service to others is complete, the incarnated portion of the soul begins the journey home. There are times when the return home is delayed, but it is never stopped.

If a soul chose a life plan that was very traumatic, one that involved considerable pain and torment, which impacts the emotional, mental, or physical body, or a mixture of each, that trauma can interfere with the direct return home.

When the "silver cord," or energetic bond, is severed between the Higher Self and the disciple at the time of physical death, the soul can become confused and feel lost. When and if this happens, the soul is then assisted by the angelics to nirvana to heal and raise their vibration for the journey home.

The Higher Self and the incarnated human are one and the same, the same soul in different bodies, with the Higher Self as the greater power.

How could we do anything else but return to our own self? What soul would want a part of itself roaming around the cosmos, lost and forgotten? Would a soul really forget about a part of itself and just continue merrily about its business without giving a thought to its Starseed? Our Higher Self is about love and compassion; it is always with us and guides us through our journey of life.

A great many people have acquired a belief that death is the end, it is scary, and it is to be feared. The truth is that death is but a transition. A soul may experience suffering and pain during its life—if that is what they chose—but the death, the transition, is painless. It is like shedding an old coat that is no longer useful. It is not the end, but the beginning!

During the preparation of our sacred life plan, we choose our exit just as we choose our karma and all our experiences during that journey. We are from the stars, and that is where we will return—to the Heavenworlds, Mother/Father God, our Higher Self, and our star families in the higher dimensions. It is cause for celebration, not fear. When we accept this truth, freedom from fear will result.

O*ur Tools*

We all have stressful times. Life happens, and then we stray from our chosen path and often allow ego to rear its bold head. Anxiety, guilt, self-blame, and self-judgment develop, followed by fear, which leads to anger toward someone or something. Those dark times of despair and sadness cause guilt or resentment to surface, and often, we chastise ourselves for not being perfect.

I believe this happens more often than we are comfortable with, so I would like to offer some solutions. Spirituality is not complicated; it is so simple. But it can be difficult to live the life we all would like to live, which is in the vibrations of love, peace, and happiness.

I am not immune to the little trips down the road of melancholy. Most of us experience those times; we work hard at doing our best, and then, "Whoops, I goofed again!" That is when we need to go back to our tools, the basics, to the very rudiments of spirituality.

These methods to get us back on track have been covered in other parts of this book, but my belief is that we tend to forget about them, so here they are again:

MEDITATION

Meditation is one of the best tools at our disposal, powerful and free of charge! Sitting in solitude and silence allows the flow of peace and serenity. It calms our emotional body, soothes the soul, and generally is a good all-around practice.

Some time ago, after experiencing a problematic issue, I took a step back from the situation, went to my meditation room, and sat in silence and contemplation. Before long, I felt the beginnings of peace, like a soft, warm blanket being draped over me. The tension slowly left my shoulders and upper back, and soon clarity and understanding of the issue materialized. All was well.

AURA CLEARING

This is a great exercise to do when your energy feels scattered or you just feel out of sorts for no apparent reason. Usually, it means your auric field is "ruffled" (perhaps you were out shopping around a lot of people and picking up on the stress of others). This is a good time to call upon Archangel Metatron and ask him to clear your auric field. He is always willing, available, and very good at it! I feel it is appropriate to say thank you to him when he has completed the process.

CHAKRA CLEARING

Sometimes we forget about these wonderful coils of energy within our body that need maintenance now and then. There are various ways to do this. None are wrong; all are effective and necessary on a regular basis. Here are a few ways to clear your chakras:

- Go into a quiet room, stand or sit, and hold the intention to clear, clean, and balance these vital energies. Make a connection with Spirit by asking them to join you and then envision a beam of white light descending from above, coming into your crown, slowly going down through your body to each chakra, all the while holding your intention.
- Connect with your Higher Self and ask her/him to assist in clearing and cleaning each chakra.
- Weather permitting, stand outdoors at first light or sunset and imagine the light from the sun

going through your body, cleaning, clearing, and replenishing each chakra.

CORD CUTTING

This can be done by yourself using your intention, but I always like to call on Spirit. It makes me feel good! I call on Archangel Michael to help me with this one. He uses his Sword of Truth to cut through the cords that may be draining vital energy from the body.

Sometimes when we are around others—family, friends, or strangers—they unconsciously send out energetic cords that will often stay attached. We are usually not aware of this and will often wonder what is making us feel so gloomy. That siphoning of our energy can cause irritability and other negative emotions.

MANTRAS

Mantras are great for increasing our energy, and there are many wonderful ones to choose from. Reciting these powerful words causes mind and heart expansion. In numerology, the number three represents the Trinity—mind–body–spirit harmony—so it's a good thing to repeat mantras at least three times. I have cited a few, but there are many others.

- I Am the Light.
  I Am the Love.
  I Am the Truth.
  I Am.
- Chant OM either aloud or silently within yourself. OM is the cosmic vibration of God within Creation. It is the mantra of eternity, a healing chant. You can find examples of how to chant OM on the Internet.
- Saying and knowing this truth can help us realize that we are most certainly masters of our own destiny:

    I and only I am in charge of
    and responsible for my
    thoughts, words, deeds, and emotions.
    No one else.
    It is called self-mastery.

CONNECTING WITH YOUR HIGHER SELF

This one is listed last, but it is not the least. Connecting with your Higher Self is immensely important. When there is any issue with an incarnated soul, or even if there is not an issue, connecting with your Higher Self is fundamental and crucial to your evolvement and to your chosen journey.

I regard that connection as my lifeline, my "everything," and it is. A disciple can connect with and talk to their Higher Self, ask questions, and ask for help or guidance at any time, day or night. The answers don't always come instantly; it all depends on what the soul agreement is, but the connection is still of major importance.

Going back to our basics may seem unimportant, and some folks may feel they have advanced beyond those basics, but it is all a matter of choice. If these reminders are helpful to just one soul, then I have accomplished what I set out to do.

The Bigger Picture

"The bigger picture" means being able to look beyond the obvious; it means taking a step back and seeing the situation from an objective point of view. Details of circumstances are important, but when the focus is on the details and not on the end result, then the goal becomes unclear.

Humanity is on the cusp of a New Dawn, a New Age, a new everything. The world around us is in constant change, as that is the way of Creation, ever changing through birth, growth, and death, whether it be humans, plants, animals, planets, suns, or Creation Itself.

Our planet is in the process of completing a cycle, also known as an age. A complete astrological cycle is approximately 26,000 years, containing within it twelve ages. The last such age we know as the Piscean Age, which was approximately 0–2000 AD.

The Age of Pisces is referred to as a vertical structure of hierarchy and power, where the controllers of humanity sit at the top and then the levels move on downward to the least fortunate—the homeless, the poor, and the abused. And that is what has been the situation on Terah for millions of years under a patriarchal society.

We are slowly moving into a New Age, the Age of Aquarius, which will be approximately another 2,000 years: 2000–4000 AD. All years are approximate, and they do overlap somewhat.

The New Age is about information, technology, networks, knowledge, and a rise in the collective consciousness. It is more even, balanced, equal, and horizontal than the Age of Pisces. It is an age of revelation, revealing that which has been kept hidden. Nothing is secret anymore, all information is available, and it's all breaking open and breaking down. The old paradigms will soon be gone, heralding the newness that is on the horizon.

The end of an astrological cycle is a very powerful time for a planet. Gaia chose to complete Her cycle by transitioning from the third dimension to the fifth dimension, known as Ascension. When this happens, a planet will go through a great cleansing and clearing, like a detoxification.

A planet usually cleanses itself through cataclysmic events, geophysical changes affecting oceans, land, and air. When the cleansing is over, often very little of the old world remains, making way for a new, fresh beginning. Gaia opted for a different method of cleansing, a kinder, gentler method, by taming down the geophysical events such as earthquakes, typhoons, and tsunamis. She chose to ascend with her inhabitants because of her great love for every sentient being living here.

In this way, humanity could also play a part in the ascension process by raising their own vibration to the ascension level of the fifth dimension, which in turn raises the vibration of Gaia, assisting in her clearing process. If Gaia had gone through the usual planetary cleansing, humanity and the various kingdoms upon her body would have endured much suffering, and there would have been tremendous destruction worldwide.

There is a time overlap when one age is over and a planet moves into the next one, and so we are experiencing the energies of two different ages. This overlap of varying energies creates confusion, disorder, and global unrest on a planet, which can continue for many years.

We as a planet and as a species are undergoing massive change as we move into the New Age of Aquarius, and those changes can be and are very difficult to live through for many. We do have choices: we can live in light and love, ride it out, celebrate our victories, and utilize the opportunity for growth, or we can feel negative.

There are those who feel like victims. No one here is a victim because we are responsible for the present situation.

We desired change, and change is happening. The very constructs of our society were built on a weak foundation that cannot sustain itself any longer.

Our society must undergo extensive transformation, and that requires monumental change and is a lengthy, complicated task. Transformation is a painful, sometimes messy process and will continue to be until it is completed. Associations and institutions such as financial, religious, industrial, medical, pharmaceutical, farming, education, and others, all need to be reformed.

During this time of transformation and massive change, humanity's task is to work within the parameters of peace, calm, acceptance, and unity rather than judgment and separation and then come from the heart in thoughts, words, and actions.

We have the choice to reflect on our lives, the way we see others, and the way we see ourselves. It is a time to think about the way we live and how we can change what no longer works for us. It is a time to remember that we came here to be a part of ascension as a collective, and that requires generating a mentality of oneness for all. It is a time to think about what is important is life, and what we want our new world to look like. The time is now.

The Three States of Mind

Human beings have within their physical bodies three states of mind: the superconscious mind, the conscious mind, and the subconscious mind.

The superconscious mind is our Higher Self, who has access to our conscious mind and our subconscious mind. For incarnated souls, the pathway from the conscious mind to the superconscious is only accessible through the heart, through love and the desire to make that connection.

The conscious mind is like a computer. It is only as smart as the data (the information) that is programmed into it. Our conscious mind has access to the superconscious but does not have *full* access to the subconscious mind.

There is a relationship between the conscious and the subconscious mind. The subconscious can express itself through the conscious mind, but that is just the surface area. There are deep, deep areas of the subconscious that the conscious mind is not prepared to contemplate, and the Higher Self *must* be present for that to happen.

We have tools available that can be utilized to attain this access, some of which are hypnosis and various healing techniques such as tapping or Reiki. If the Higher Self deems the time is right and if it is in our soul agreement for that access, then she/he will allow it.

The subconscious mind is a storage place for information. The subconscious mind does not have access to the conscious or the superconscious mind. Stored within the subconscious mind lies the truth, the truth of who we really are: galactic beings wearing a human mantle.

Also stored in the subconsciousness are our memories of home, memories of where we really came from, memories of past lives and all the realities we have experienced on our various journeys through countless lifetimes.

When we experience trauma or negativity in a lifetime and the hurt is great, we tuck it away in the subconsciousness because it hurts too much to keep it in our conscious mind, where we can easily access it at any time. And there it sits, deeply buried, and waits to be released.

The subconscious mind is also used by the superconsciousness to store information, where that, too, sits and waits for just the right time to be brought forward by the Higher Self and utilized. When we are ready, he/she will present that information to the conscious mind for us to use. Our paths are guided with precision, and no mistakes are ever made; our Higher Self is the divine director of our preplanned great drama of life.

Our Higher Self also watches and waits for the right time to allow us to clear any deep-seated, buried hurts and negativity of present or past life trauma that is stored in the subconscious. When we have reached a particular phase of our life path determined by the Higher Self, she/he will bring that negative energy up for clearing, and she/he will assist in that process.

The past life memories that we buried are stored in the cells of our bodies for us to work with in the present, guided by the Higher Self. It is like karma; if it has happened here in the past or present, then it must be dealt with here. It cannot be cleared in any other reality. It is our own karmic energy, which we generated with Self. Since we are unable to access our subconscious mind, we need the Higher Self. This is not the only reason to connect with our greater power, but it is a very important part of our evolution to do so.

Clearing stored negative energy is a soul choice. There is no judgment meted out nor any rush to do anything; all we really have to do is just *be*. Every soul has a different path each incarnation, and there are no requirements. We all have the gift of free will. Since we are eternal beings and have eternity to work on our spiritual progress, we are free to evolve as we choose.

Cosmic Exchange

M ost souls on Terah are here to learn, expand their consciousness, and balance karma. Occasionally, any one of those three choices can involve difficulty, and it is not always an easy task to advance in evolution.

There is a term often used called "cosmic exchange." I love those words; I believe they carry a powerful impact! I have learned through experience that an incarnation can sometimes be complex and rocky; it can also be wonderfully rewarding.

The key is to discover the way of the cosmos, determine how it all works in the higher dimensions, and that discovery may take a variety of intricate pathways that we all need to learn how to navigate. It is worth it, because along the way we can take huge leaps forward in consciousness and feel the joy of completing a task that we set for ourselves.

We each have the opportunity to become victorious and then celebrate those victories. It all depends on how dedicated and determined we are. The way to higher consciousness involves extensive inner work, and that means going within and clearing out all the baggage we have accumulated over time, as well as solidifying our energetic connection to Spirit.

Occasionally, that baggage can be hidden deep within our subconscious mind, and that is when we need the assistance of our Higher Self to release and clear anything and everything that no longer serves us. Sometimes we are not aware of the extra load we are carrying, and sometimes we are aware of it and just ignore it. Those burdens can hold us back from the wonders and magic of the exciting and mystical world of a Starseed.

Our task as disciples also involves ridding ourselves of antiquated beliefs and negative attitudes that we have acquired through living in this density. One of the main reasons we chose this planet is because of the numerous challenges that we are constantly faced with. A good way to cope with and manage the challenges is to be mindful of our thoughts, words, and actions; by living daily in our "now".

When we take the time and make the effort to work toward our own evolutionary advancement, we often experience a feeling of joy, a feeling of accomplishment of a "job well done", a feeling and a knowing that we have worked hard and attained the desired result, which is most often a rise in consciousness. We have earned it and that is cause for celebration!

The Ring Pass Not

Those souls on the spiritual path of consciously searching the vast unknown, also known as the metaphysical and the paranormal, are constantly striving to attain spiritual growth. There are lessons to learn along the way that are required for the growth to happen.

The lessons are not always easy, and that can be due to a force in our lives called the "ring pass not." We all have a ring pass not, which is there to ensure that we learn and experience everything that is included in our life plan, everything that we chose to learn and experience before we can advance to a higher level of consciousness. All those situations are directed by our Higher Self, and no step can be missed.

Incarnation and evolution are both a step-by-step process, and in order to proceed to the next step, cycle, or phase, we must first complete the one we are presently occupying.

It is similar to a room, an area, or a field that cannot be passed through until we have overcome or learned all that is in the room. When that is accomplished, we are allowed to open a new door and explore a new room, then another, and another. We all have self-imposed limitations such as old beliefs, attitudes, fears, ego, lack of confidence, and past life trauma that can, and often do, hold us back.

We cannot earn the right to gain more experiences until we have released and overcome the limitations in our present circle, ring, or area. Karma plays a big part of our ring pass not, and if our soul agreement was to balance such karma, then that is what we must do. If we choose truth, compassion, love, and acceptance in each situation we encounter, then our journey becomes much smoother.

Each soul has her or his own journey and lessons, so each one's ring pass not, is different. Existing on a planet of duality creates more effort to accomplish our chosen goals in life, but it is worth it.

Our Crystalline Body

Would the Mother Goddess create a new human, a perfect human body, with the predisposition for rapid spiritual enlightenment and then just allow that perfect body to be *genetically corrupted*? The answer is no, She would not allow that to happen. Everything that is happening, has happened, and will happen is all by divine plan. There was a built-in backup system, and that backup is the crystalline body. The implementation of the backup system is under the guidance of the Mother Goddess, Archangel Gaia, the Being that is the consciousness of our planet.

The situation on this planet regarding the global pandemic and the ensuing vaccine was known long ago in the higher dimensions. We as souls knew what was in our future before we chose to come here. Due to the necessity of the Veil of Forgetfulness, we have forgotten, but many are coming into their awareness and waking up to the truth.

The purpose of the manipulation of a perfectly normal virus within the human body was to have an excuse to create a "cure" in the form of a vaccine. The purpose of the vaccine was to kill a portion of humanity for population control and to *genetically corrupt the DNA* of those surviving the poison of the vaccine. Through divine will, this was not permitted to happen.

The severity of the vaccine has been modified so it cannot cause the damage that was initially intended by those who created it. The corruption of the virus and the creation of a vaccine that was forced on humanity has resulted in many souls exiting the planet. Those most affected were the ones with underlying health issues, and their transition was a soul choice.

This is how the backup plan unfolded:

It all began the moment the great plan came into being eons ago. But for this writing, I will start at the beginning of the twentieth century. That was when Gaia put out her clarion call for help because this planet and humanity were on the brink of destruction due to the abuse that occurred over millions of years to the planet itself and to humanity.

Archangel Gaia has incarnated many times for millions of years, working to raise the vibration of Earth. As a soul in the higher dimensions, she has free will, as does any soul. Using her free will, she has chosen to become an inhabitant of Earth to work side by side with humanity toward the common goal of complete liberation from the dark forces. Through her many incarnations, Archangel Gaia has anchored the goddess energies into the very heart of the planet, and those love energies have encompassed and infused planet Earth, creating great change, and they will continue to do so.

Countless souls answered Archangel Gaia's call for help by incarnating as Starseeds numerous times, and for these souls, it was and is a win-win situation. It works two ways. We as Starseeds help uplift the energy of Gaia, and in so doing, we are able to achieve much forward progress in evolution.

When the new human was created, there were activation codes built within our DNA as a major part of the backup plan. These crucial codes are being activated at precisely the right time, and it is an ongoing process. We are still receiving some of those activation codes at this time. They are important because those activations are largely responsible for the great many people who are in the process of "waking up" now—waking up to the truth of who we really are and where we come from.

As we evolve and raise our level of consciousness, our DNA changes from carbon to crystalline. *The crystalline body is impervious to genetic corruption.* We, in truth, are masters of our own destiny; we have the free will to change our DNA through our desire and willingness to connect with Spirit. By reaching out and making that energetic connection, we raise our vibration, thus increasing the Light within us.

The Light is the crystalline. The more Light we embrace and hold, the more our DNA changes to become crystalline. The Light is immune to disease, to noxious chemicals in our air, food, water, and anything else in our environment that can corrupt our DNA.

We have been propped up from those in the higher dimensions as well—from the divine, from the Galactic Federation of Worlds, and from the angelic realm. We have received aid from the divine in the form of huge influxes of energy from the great, central sun, Alcyone, which is filtered through our own sun, Sol, then sent on to us as solar flares. We are also receiving photonic energy from the Photon Belt and Porlana C energy from the Galactic Federation of Worlds, as well as guidance and support from them and the angelic realm. This is just a summary of the extensive amount of help we really do receive.

In the early 1920s, millions of souls chose to come here to help Gaia. They were known as the indigo children because of their distinct indigo aura, which corresponds to the sixth chakra, the chakra of intuition, vision, clarity, truth, and that of a spiritual defender.

This era was called the roaring twenties. It was around the time the first world war ended, and people were ready for something new, something exciting, something different. In the unconscious mind, they knew it was a special time and realized that change was needed. That was not a conscious knowing by most until almost a century later. Now. There are still indigo children alive today, and they are continuing their effort toward liberation. They were, and are, known as the Way-showers, clearing the way for those who incarnated after them.

Next to emerge were the rainbow children, arriving in the 1950's. They came in with an upgraded chakra system aligned with all the light frequencies, all the colors of the rainbow (thus, the "rainbow children"). They are the game changers, the nonconformists, not normally following the status quo; they prepare their own way. In the 1960s, they were recognized as the "flower children" or "hippies." They are idealists and advocates of love and peace. They became known as "the founders of change," touting their own rules and forging new roads for those who would follow.

At the beginning of the new millennium (early 2000s), the crystal children arrived and graced us with their gentleness, their loving ways, and their intense desire for peace. They arrived with the purpose of making this world a better place. They are the peacemakers; they are very spiritual and here to bring love, light, and joy to those around them.

Each new group of souls has brought with them many spiritual gifts and left their own imprint on the planet and on others. As the incarnated disciple works to move forward in evolution through love and desire for peace, they contribute and support the advancement of the crystalline body.

The group that will incarnate next are called the diamond children, so named for the attributes they will come in with. They will have the strength and endurance to hold the consistency of the Truth. The world will need the diamond children, for they will be the ones who will be able to hold and sustain all that was accomplished by so many before them. They will solidify the changes that are coming, and they will sparkle and shine as brightly as the diamond that they are named after.

Karma

Karma is one of the most misunderstood words, and situation, that disciples encounter on their spiritual journey.

There is no "good" or "bad" karma. Karma is simply an action. It is an energy generated by free will action through thoughts, words, or deeds.

It is a perfect example of the Universal Law of Cause and Effect. The action (the cause) creates the consequences (the effect).

We are all responsible for our thoughts, words, and deeds; no one else.

Our souls are eternal, and each soul has experienced numerous incarnations. During those incarnations, we all create both positive and negative energy, which is often left unfinished upon our transition back to the higher realms. This unfinished energy is known as karma.

Does karma have to be balanced? The answer is no. There is no requirement by anyone to balance karma; it is a soul choice. The other side of the statement is that negative energy that is created and left unfinished, unbalanced, or uncleared will hinder our evolutionary progress. Knowing this truth usually prods the aspirant to balance past or present energy.

When an energy has been created on a particular planet, it must be balanced on that planet. It cannot be balanced on a different planet or in the higher dimensions.

Many souls have chosen to complete all past and present karma in this lifetime during the massive ascension process of Gaia and humanity because a soul cannot ascend with unfinished karma. Ascension in the physical means reaching a fifth-dimensional level of awareness, and a soul cannot come into that level of consciousness while holding onto unfinished karma.

The decision to balance karma or not is included in the earth life plan. After incarnating, the process is directed by the Higher Self and carried out by the disciple. All past and present life experiences foster the ascension, meaning these experiences add to and enable the aspirant to reach ascension.

It is not a complicated process; however, it can be, and very often is, difficult. In order to balance karma, one must have the desire to do so and then go forward with a pure heart. It's about self-love, self-forgiveness, love, and forgiving another soul and accepting the path of that soul.

$\int$he Kundalini

The kundalini is an equal balance of the divine feminine and the divine masculine energies. There is great mystery and curiosity around this energy force because of the power contained within it. It is the ultimate life force.

Kundalini, in the language of Sanskrit, means "coiled one" and is most often portrayed as a snake figure. It is latent energy located at the base of the spine in all humans and lies dormant until it is time to awaken, a time that is determined by the Higher Self.

When activated, kundalini flows or undulates from the base of the spine in a serpent-like motion on an upward trajectory toward the crown chakra. As the kundalini energy moves upward, it goes through all chakras, giving each an upgrade, which then causes them to become more stabilized and efficient. When the chakras work more efficiently, pain and disease diminish, which gives the aspirant more freedom to pursue the metaphysical world, and that can result in consciousness expansion.

The Higher Self will direct his/her aspirant as they see fit. Guidance will be there for each one who is actively working toward spiritual awareness. As with all spiritual work, the task of the Seeker is to tune in to the guidance that is so readily available.

When curiosity develops regarding the kundalini, this means that it is already activated and ready to start the upward passage through the body. It will rise through the natural unfoldment of consciousness advancement. Meditation, connecting with Spirit, and other spiritual practices, such as yoga and chanting mantras, will aid in the flow of energy. The rising of the kundalini can take several lifetimes or just one lifetime, depending on the soul decision.

There are souls who desire to force the activation and upward motion through artificial means. Although this can be successful in some situations, it is not recommended by those in the higher dimensions. If activation is forced through artificial means, it will not necessarily stay risen because of the level of consciousness that is present in the disciple at the time of the unnatural or artificial method used.

If induced, it will only rise short of the heart chakra, usually staying in the root area. This is because the forcing of the kundalini is instigated by the dark forces, and if an aspiring Seeker takes that road, then there must be healing and inner work carried out to correct the misstep.

The goal of the rising of the kundalini is to reach the crown chakra. Once there, a merging takes place between these two mighty forces, and something is born within the individual—much like a child being born. It's akin to a new being born within.

When kundalini reaches the crown, it continues to rise and ultimately connects one to their divinity. Once the kundalini is active and risen to the crown, it remains active throughout the physical body, circulating up and down through the chakras and the auric field if the disciple continues to follow the Path to Enlightenment.

The beautiful and profound action of kundalini awakening has various effects on all four bodies, which include enhanced creativity, a higher level of consciousness, and a greater connection with the universe and cosmic consciousness. The potential for spiritual advancement is huge, which is why so many disciples are interested in the kundalini.

$\mathcal{D}$ensity and Dimensions

T hese two terms can sometimes cause confusion within the spiritual community. They are often used synonymously, though there is a difference. They are not the same. The short explanation is:

- Density—the vibrational frequency of matter
- Dimension—a level of awareness

The universe, multiverse, or omniverse holds within it countless dimensions, and within each dimension are thirteen layers, or densities. Each density vibrates at a different frequency, meaning a different rate of speed. Creation is energy. Everything in existence is energy. Energy is eternal; it can change form, but it will never cease to exist.

DENSITY

The most basic life forms are water and minerals. They do have a consciousness, and the matter they are comprised of vibrates at the first frequency, therefore, they are known as the first density.

The plant and animal kingdoms operate from the second density, meaning their molecular makeup is vibrating at level two frequency. They, too, have a consciousness, although they do not possess an ego, an awareness of self.

Next on the evolutionary ladder are those of the third density, who possess self-awareness known as ego. This is the density where humans begin. Those of the third density do have self-awareness, can remember the past, are cognizant of the future, and are able to feel separation. There are more densities, but for this writing, the focus is on the first, second, and third.

DIMENSIONS

A dimension is a level of awareness. It is not a place to go physically; it is a state of consciousness. I once heard it described this way: "Dimensions are the lens through which you perceive reality, or the way in which you define your reality."

The confusion arises because we can be in the same density and dimension simultaneously or we can be living in one density and have a different level of awareness, meaning that we can be living in the third density while consciously operating in the fifth dimension. We can live *in* a certain density, but we do not have to be *of* that density.

Those souls who are operating at a very high (fifth and above) level of consciousness cannot comfortably live in the lower densities. When the difference between the two—density and dimension—becomes too great, a soul cannot survive in it.

We go forward from one dimensional level to another through the heart. If we are operating in the fourth dimension and wish to move up, we must learn to manage our ego, learn that the most powerful force in creation is love, learn unity consciousness, and, of course, remember who we are and where we come from.

$\mathcal{T}$imelines

What is a timeline?
How is it relevant to spiritual growth?

How can we as aspiring Starseeds use timelines to advance along the spiritual path?

There are various ways to describe timelines. Here are a few:

- A timeline is a pathway you choose to follow in your life. However, throughout your life, you have the freedom to change timelines whenever you choose.
- A timeline is wherever we place our awareness.
- It is the possibility of a certain occurrence.

There are different timelines that have different outcomes. For example: there can be a number of souls who can agree on a certain timeline, but the timeline depends on the consciousness that you need to possess in order to operate on that timeline.

The earth is now on a timeline of the New Age. It has taken hundreds of years and a terrific amount of effort to get here. The Lightworkers who have incarnated on this planet now have pulled the earth onto the timeline of the New Age of Brotherhood and Unity because of their conscious match with that timeline.

The focus of many souls to accomplish a certain goal—which in our case is the complete breakdown of the upper echelon of a corrupt society—is a very powerful energy.

Our society was built on a weak foundation of power and greed by those in control, and therefore it cannot sustain itself. It must fall. The old paradigms must collapse and be replaced by those of the higher vibrations, such as love, compassion, acceptance, and truth.

Some people ask if it's possible to change a timeline. The answer is yes. If you consider a timeline as a pathway, it is similar to walking along a trail. The trail that you are currently walking on represents your present timeline. At any time, a fork might appear along the trail. When you reach that point, you have the choice: continue to follow the present path or change directions.

You have the free will to choose any fork in the road you wish. If your desire is to attain spiritual growth, then you do that by consciously increasing your vibration and following a newer, higher pathway.

"Jumping timelines" simply means you move from one direction, path, or timeline to another. However, you must have the consciousness of that timeline in order to operate on it.

There is a connection between consciousness and timelines. Your level of consciousness depends upon which timeline you choose to follow. In order to advance in consciousness, one must always choose a higher vibratory timeline.

*O*ur Multidimensional Self

B eing a spiritual person has numerous advantages, and one of those is the awakening process. Spiritual awakening is when we shed the Veil of Forgetfulness and come into the realization of who we are and where we come from. We are galactic beings inhabiting human bodies. That knowledge then opens the door to more knowledge as the quest for full enlightenment continues.

As I progressed along my own path, I often read or heard the term "the multidimensional self" and thought it was a very interesting group of words, but I was not quite sure of the true meaning. Eventually I received clarity, and I would like to share that knowledge with you.

- Multi—means many or multiple
- Dimensional—means level of awareness

Our multidimensional self is the multiple levels of awareness that our consciousness experiences during the lifetime. It can also be described as the ego, aspects of self, or multidimensional self; they are all the same.

We are more than we can imagine, more than we think or believe we are. There are numerous parts (aspects or ego) that make up who and what we really are.

These parts are the result of our beliefs, and our beliefs are the result of our five senses. Our beliefs are the product of what we acquired through the educational systems, religion, mainstream media, our parents, and our society in general.

We have been taught that the leaders of our organizations, such as governments, medical providers, schools, churches, among others, all know more than we do. We have given away our innate power, the power we were born with, and the power of who we really are, has been buried beneath societal pressure and misinformation.

During the awakening process, our level of consciousness increases, and we begin the journey toward the knowledge of our multidimensionality. We are accustomed to only using our main (or most known) five senses, which are sight, sound, smell, taste, and touch, and these five senses normally create our reality, but when we think "outside the box," we can go much further. We can expand our consciousness and then encompass and hold more dimensions of self.

It is truly amazing when we awaken to the truth of our own power, the truth of the many aspects of self, the many states of awareness that we enjoy. It's just a matter of stretching ourselves, stretching our imagination to think beyond the usual, beyond the five senses that generally make up our reality.

We are accustomed to identifying as only a singular consciousness on a daily basis, the one where we employ the usual five senses, but we are much more than that. There is another state of consciousness that can be called "multiple consciousness"—the state of having multiple senses of self within a single awareness.

Through working toward a higher level of evolution, we have the ability to occupy multiple levels of awareness within a single consciousness, meaning that there's another consciousness where you can hold more than one soul impulse. With this awareness, we can bi-locate, or occupy two or more places at once—not in the physical, but with our consciousness.

As our consciousness rises, we become aware of the multidimensional selves within one consciousness; that means dimensions within dimensions. We become aware that we encompass, hold, and occupy multiple dimensions of multiple selves.

With one level of consciousness, you can feel joy and pleasure experiencing a beautiful sunset while, at the same time, another level of self can be irritated with another person who perhaps showed you disrespect in some area, or you can be thinking of your grocery list or how to best manage a child who is upset at something. You have the ability to do all of this, to "be" all of this, to be in various dimensions (levels of awareness) at the same time.

Here's another example: You project your awareness to planning a party while you are driving your vehicle down a busy street. You can stay on your side of the road, stop at the red light, and go when it turns green, all the while thinking of your upcoming social gathering.

There may be times when you will "hear" that silent voice within your head utter a phrase, a comment that seems foreign to you and at the same time feels familiar. You ask yourself, *Was that me or someone else? Is there someone else inside my head? Who is this someone else?* You may think, *Who would say that to me?* or *Who is that inside my head?* Well, it is very likely one of your selves! The awakening process can, and very often does, cause confusion, and to offset that, it also causes excitement! There is always balance.

Someone once said to me, "Confusion can be good; it means you are about to grow."

So, hang on, enjoy the ride, and take what comes your way with joy in your heart!

When you really think about the true "you" and the many facets of self, you will realize how wonderful the human body and soul truly are!

Connecting the Dots

Spirituality is fascinating, from my point of view. Recently, I had a conversation with a member of one of my groups. This Seeker had a question regarding timelines, and during my explanation, I realized how we are connected, not just to each other but within our very own special life plans!

There is an affiliation between timelines, multidimensionality, density, dimensions, karma, and kundalini. They are all connected. We often think of these aspects of our journey as separate, but they are not. Each is a huge part of the path of a Starseed and necessary to development and evolution.

As they intermingle, one affects the other in numerous ways. I find the association between timelines and multidimensionality a very close one. We can and do move forward, backward, and between timelines. Then there are "merging timelines." Merging timelines is when the timelines come together.

That happens when we bring together the various aspects of self, the aspects of our multidimensionality. Each aspect of self can be operating in a different dimension as explained in "Our Multidimensional Self." When we merge or "gather" these aspects of self, it causes the timelines to merge. It all comes together.

I heard someone mention "the gathering" a few years ago, and at that time, I thought it meant gathering of like-minded souls or gathering of soul groups or families. It can and often does indicate that, but it also means merging our multidimensional selves, because we are gathering those parts of self together. It is a crucial part of the ascension process.

The merging of selves and timelines can be different for each incarnate. Each journey is different, and so is the ascension process. It all depends on the soul choice; it is included in the prelife plan.

The Dance of Life

"Listen to the music of the Spheres
for it will take you Home"

~ Lord Adrigon

Dance of Life, what does it mean? Life can show us many different steps as we dance along our path to the beat of our hearts, the beat of our minds, and sometimes to the beat of others' hearts and minds. This is not always a bad thing to do. It allows us to be flexible in our daily lives.

The steps of our dance with life can be tricky, hard to follow, and, occasionally, downright confusing! This is when we need to learn the steps slowly and proceed carefully so that if we do stumble, we are able to pick up the beat again and move along with the music. It is important to dance to the beat of the universe, to the spheres, and to the heartbeat of Creation, as this will ease our way.

There are times when we will take two steps forward and one step back, depending on what the dance requires. It is wise to listen to the tempo of the music and follow the beat, for if we are "out of time" with the tempo, challenges will arise. If we stay in step with what life offers us, then all goes smoothly.

The tempo can change at any moment, so we must be ready to change as well. The best way for the dance of life to go smoothly is to be adaptable, able to move to the varying energies and situations, whether they are slow and seductive, fast and furious, light as a fairy, or smooth as the waters of a pond on a calm day.

Sometimes we have a partner in this dance of life, and sometimes we dance alone. If we have a partner, it is not unusual to trip over their feet if we as a couple are out of sync. Learning the steps of our partner is as important as learning them for ourselves, as this is paramount to smooth dancing.

When the music stops, it is the exhilaration of the dance and the reward at the conclusion of it that keeps us going and makes it all worthwhile. So, join me in this dance; dance with me through this lifetime. Dance with commitment, determination, your own power, joy, hope, peace, and love! We will make beautiful music together, as one.

Higher Self and the Ship

My Higher Self is my captain. The ship is me. This higher part of myself is ever present, my constant companion and my power. She guides me through calm seas, choppy waters, gales, and the instability that is life.

When the waters are rough and treacherous and I careen wildly, she is ever steady at the helm, navigating the tumultuous waves, incarnation after incarnation. After the storms pass, we glide smoothly and silently through the calmness that ensues. Every now and then, we encounter the Veil of Fog, and that is when we maneuver cautiously.

When the winds of change billow through my sails, my Higher Self is my loving, constant support and mainstay. Occasionally, I veer off course, and when this occurs, she is at my side with her amazing tolerance, patience, and love to gently but firmly show me the way back.

My captain is all-knowing and ever vigilant as, together, we traverse the sometimes turbulent passage through life—her love is of such purity and great depth that it is indescribable. One day, when we gaze at the horizon, we will behold the Light and know we are at the place where the earth and sky meet—the physical and the spiritual.

We are almost home.

My Higher Self is my guide through eternity, and I am infinitely grateful to have her by my side!

MY GUARDIAN ANGEL —
REAL WORLD OR ILLUSION

August 28, 2017

Greetings to all, it is our joy to connect with you in this way. There is some confusion regarding angels, guides, and guardian angels. You all have your very own guardian angel who has been with you since your soul was first cast. This angel never, ever leaves you. You have other angels and guides who come and go according to what is going on in your life at a specific time.

There is no trick to connecting with us. We are always available and ready to assist in any way that we are permitted within the limits of Universal Law. You just need to ask, make the effort, and presto, there we are! Simple but powerful knowledge to have. The key to connecting with us is to listen to your intuition.

You are receiving messages constantly—we send you information in the form of energy, and this translates into your own thoughts. Sometimes, you think you have come up with a great idea, but that just might be your guides and angels sending you this idea. Heed your inner voice, follow your guidance, and trust your intuition.

There are many questions asked about your journey and your present incarnation—we will simplify and shed some light on the subject in this way:

Think of the room that you occupy as your home world and think of yourselves as eager Starseeds yearning for something new and exciting. You have explored every nook and cranny of this world; you have searched every closet, opened every door, and now you are ready for more. You choose to venture outside your own home world, outside of your comfort zone.

You gather your friends and family and tell them of your decision. Some of them decide to follow your example. Plans are made down to the finest detail, contracts are signed, agreements are forged between other souls, and it becomes a huge enterprise of hope, eagerness, love, and desire to learn new lessons and to assist beings in other worlds. Approval is granted for your life plan.

There is a catch to this plan, which is that you must forget your life in the stars and travel this journey unaware of your previous life. Soon you are ready, and off you go on your adventure. As you leave your home world, your memory of all that you are, all that you know—including your connection to and knowledge of Spirit—is erased.

You must adjust your level of consciousness to that of the planet you chose, and as you descend into this new life, you truly do begin anew.

You become the actor who will play out your great plan, and your drama begins to unfold. You may have selected a life of luxury, homelessness, addiction, teaching, healing, volunteering, or perhaps just "being," spreading your light in this way. Earth is a planet of duality, so there is much to learn and numerous opportunities for soul advancement.

The lessons and challenges are plentiful, and you occasionally stumble along the way. This can be a good thing, as there are no mistakes, only lessons to learn and soul growth to achieve. What you may consider a "mistake" can be an opportunity for growth. You have much assistance from many Beings of Light, friends who stayed back to support you, and loving guidance from your Higher Self.

One day, you notice a restlessness, and you feel unsettled. You are not comfortable with your life and feel that something is amiss. This is because you are feeling the stirrings of awakening, and your Higher Self is urging you to listen to your inner self, your heart. You become a Seeker and realize that there is something more than what you know and understand as life in your world.

You spend years searching for truth, and when you find it, you know that you have found that which you seek. You realize that your life here is a drama, that you are the actor, and that none of it is real. It is all an illusion. Your real world is back where you come from, the stars.

Some years go by, and you become weary. You know that your time on this planet is soon over. You know that when you finally go home, you will be met by many loving beings waiting for you with open arms!

That, dear ones, is what you are experiencing from our perspective.

LORD ASHTAR

July 27, 2017

Greetings—I AM Ashtar. We bring a message to you today of hope and encouragement that will lift your spirits.

We are nearing the end, some say the End Times. That is not a bad thing; it is the end of the old and a blazing new beginning for this planet and all who occupy her. The adage is true, there is light at the end of the tunnel, the end of the tunnel being your many incarnations through various lifetimes. *You* are the Light, you and every other soul who feels the stirrings of Spirit and awakens to their true self. Your light will assist in bringing about the liberation of this planet!

Never underestimate your power. You are powerful, and the dark ones have done their best to make you forget that. You are almost through your hardships and sacrifices. We applaud you. We acknowledge your strength and endurance in the face of all that you endure on this planet as you constantly go forward despite these challenges.

You are our ground contacts, and without you, we could not accomplish the work that we do. When you put forth your effort, we magnify it, and thus are able to do our part. For this, we say a heartfelt thank you.

Yes, dear ones, the Light on this planet is increasing daily; we see the changes from our vantage point as more and more souls awaken to their true purpose—to spread the Light. You are the ones who are making the difference. The dark forces are scattering in disarray, trying desperately to hold onto their control, but it is slipping away, and they are confused—running scared, some infighting. Chaos reigns, as they know that the end of their power over this planet and its occupants is at hand.

Take heart, the final days are near. Stay strong and hold the Light, for there is much coming to you in the months ahead.

There is some fear on this planet about extraterrestrials that is generated by the dark forces—it is deliberate, and their motivation is to cause that fear and gain more control over you. *Know this*—we are benevolent beings with Creator's plan as our first goal, and we come to you with the highest vibration of love.

We have been in your skies for thousands of your years, doing what we love to do—protect, support, guide, and assist. We are many and originate from various planets throughout the galaxies. We do have among us some onlookers, those from different universes who are interested in this great endeavor of yours. They are curious to know how this mass ascension of planet and humanity is done and what the final outcome will be.

When you look up in your skies, know that we are there—cloaked, but still there. We wait and assist in whatever way that Universal Law permits, and we send you constant love!

I AM Ashtar.

LORD SANANDA (JESUS)

September 9, 2017

Dear friends, it is our great joy to bring this message to you today through this channel. We want to remind you that you are all channels: you channel love, you channel information, you channel light. Most of you are unaware of this due to the Veil that you agreed to take during this lifetime. That does not mean that those vibrations are not coming through to you; it just means that you have forgotten your higher dimensional side.

You have forgotten how truly powerful and wondrous you are. You have forgotten that you are all one, you are all connected. Think of it in this way: See yourselves as a tiny droplet in an immense body of water, a minuscule part of an ocean. You are one molecule, yet completely connected to every other molecule in that body of water. Together, you create the ocean—a beautiful, powerful force.

As you look around, you may feel alone and separate from your fellow humans, yet you are not separate. You are a part of the greater whole. When unified, you project a powerful light that overtakes the darkness. Know your power and connectedness; know you are mighty in your unity.

Before you came to this planet, you made agreements with each other, agreements with us who stayed back to guide you through your journey. You agreed to remember the love, to bring the love to those around you, and to share when you noticed someone in need.

When life presents you with challenges, you sometimes fall into the lower vibrations, and that is when we are there, loving, guiding, giving you compassion, and supporting you in every way that we are permitted.

Go forth with strength and courage, dear ones. Know that you are loved beyond measure.

I am Sananda.

THE MOTHER GODDESS

March 17, 2021

Greetings to each and every one of you. This message is a message of love, a message of hope, a message of truth. A message to help you understand the meaning of life as you know it on this planet at this time. It is known in the higher dimensions as a time of revelation, a time of readjustment, a time of cleansing, a time of renewal, regrowth, and rebirth.

We greet you with great joy and celebration, for your freedom is at hand. You have suffered mightily, and in that suffering, you have grown exponentially; you have shown your true colors; you have shown the planet, the rest of humanity, the galaxy, and, yes, the universe that you are strong. You have shown everyone that you can do it—you have done it! You have brought about change, a much-needed change, and you have worked for the life you deserve and the life you desire. It is here for you. Your time of enslavement is almost at an end. And we want you to know how proud we are of all of you, how much we applaud you, and how happy we are for you.

Yes, there are a few blips and bumps ahead, but they are minor compared to what you have already endured. You will get through the rest of these bumps as well, never forgetting that you have much assistance from so many in the higher dimensions and your own heart, because that is where you work from, that is where your truth lies, and that is where your strength is.

This is not a *you* and *us* situation. This is a *we* situation, for you are us and we are you. We are one. You are our representatives, you are the boots on the ground, and you have done the work that was required. Go forward with hope and joy in your heart, for there is smooth sailing ahead, and we are joyful to celebrate with you. We have walked side by side with you from the beginning, and you never were, are, or will be alone. We are working with you, supporting you with love, joy, and compassion, and we will continue our loving support and assistance in whatever way is possible within the guidelines of Universal Law.

In the coming weeks and months, you will be informed of various events that have transpired on your planet that may cause you consternation and disbelief. It is important to remember to practice nonjudgment when you are challenged and to remember your free will, your right to choose that which is your truth. And to remember that each soul on the planet is playing a role.

This is a planet of duality. There exists a negative and a positive force, and through that duality, you have had the opportunity to learn and grow, to attain a higher level of evolution. Without the duality, you would not have learned how to overcome adversity, how to feel such compassion for each other, how to accept your differences. That push, pull, attract, and repel is what makes everything tick. It is what enables you to move forward.

The importance of what happens on this planet is profound, for it will affect your galaxy, the universe, and beyond. You are the micro in this plan, you affect the macro, and as you move up, so does the galaxy, universe, and, yes, other souls.

With your sacrifices, your suffering, your growth and evolvement, you are giving others in the universe that same opportunity. And you are being watched and monitored. Many are learning from you as you process those energies and those situations, watching how you experience them and then process them.

You are a very, very critical part of this great plan. So, it's important that you continue as you are, that you continue showing compassion, that you continue showing acceptance, that you continue showing love, and that you continue to shine your light.

CREATOR

One beautiful, sunny day, while I was walking in the Sonoran Desert, I received a message from Creator. I was thrilled with the contact and loved the words that came to me. I wish to share those words because I believe they are profound and the truth of the message resonated with me very much.

Live in Love
Love to Live
All is One
One is All

~ Creator

Glossary

ANCIENT WISDOM: A term used to describe the knowledge that resides within us all and that we can access through the heart connection with Spirit.

ANUNNAKI: A species that occupied our planet billions of years ago that originated from a planet in the constellation Sirius.

ASCENSION: Ascension is a word used to describe movement from one dimension to another and from one plane to another; it is also called Spiritual Evolution. It is the process of moving up in levels of consciousness. Ascending in the physical means reaching the level of fifth dimension while in the physical body.

ASPIRANT: One who desires to achieve something or follow a certain path.

ATLANTIS: A massive landmass in the Atlantic Ocean situated off the coast of Africa that sank beneath the waves about 26,000 years ago.

CHAKRA: A chakra is an energy coil within our body. The seven most well-known are the root, sacral, solar plexus, heart, throat, third eye, and crown. These energy centers take in energy from the outside world, work with it, and use it to keep the internal organs functioning.

CONSTELLATION: A formation of stars.

CONSCIOUSNESS: A state of being.

DENSITY: The vibrational frequency of matter.

DIMENSION: A level of awareness.

DOWNLOAD: Information provided by our Higher Self that is sent to our subconscious mind to surface and be utilized at a given time.

FREE WILL: The gift of Prime Creator to every soul. The freedom to choose our reality without interference.

FREQUENCY: The rate at which molecules vibrate.

GALAXY: A group of star formations within the universe.

GODDESS, GOD: The first souls that were cast, cocreators with Source energy, also referred to as the Elohim. Guardians and protectors of the universes. All Gods and Goddesses are archangels, but not all archangels are Gods and Goddesses.

HIGHER SELF: The greater part of an incarnate that remained in the higher realms and the director of the path of the incarnate.

HOLY GRAIL: "Holy" is self-explanatory. "Grail" can mean cup or vessel. Archangel Ariel is known on Earth and in the higher realms as the Holy Grail, the vessel which is holy. She is the Goddess of our universe and the consciousness of our planet. Finding the Holy Grail means reaching a fifth-dimensional level of consciousness that is one with the earth, thus attaining ascension.

INCARNATE: Also known as disciple. A soul that assumes physical form and inhabits a planet.

(RE)INCARNATION: Rebirth of a soul in a physical body.

KARMA: Energy or situations, positive or negative, left unfinished during an incarnation.

KARMIC WHEEL: The incarnation of a soul again and again to complete unresolved energy.

LEMURIA: An immense continent situated in the Pacific Ocean, which sank about 26,000 years ago.

LIGHTBODY (Merkaba): The vessel the soul uses to travel. Merkaba means light, body, spirit. The Merkaba is two intersecting triangles—one masculine and one feminine—that spin in opposite directions in perfect balance. The union of these two triangles creates an energy field around the physical body. The energy field is a vehicle of protection and transportation for the soul as it travels the astral world.

LIGHTWORKER: Any soul who comes from a pure heart and shares their light with another in a kind, compassionate, loving, and caring way. He/she is one who incarnates with a tendency to be of service to others and pursues knowledge of the great unknown. One does not have to do anything to be a Lightworker. Some souls just "are," and in that way, their energy affects those around them and uplifts another energetically and spiritually.

LIGHT LANGUAGE: Light Language is a multidimensional language understood by all on a soul level. It is high-frequency encodings understood by the heart. It works on a level that causes shifts that empower, encode, and open the heart to "feel beyond the mind." It interacts instantly with the Lightbody. It is a deeply layered alchemical transmission of information and most often cannot be translated word for word.

Another explanation: Light Language is energy transmission through sacred sounds of sacred geometries patterned by light to awaken new intelligence.

MATRIX: An energy surrounding planet Earth originally placed as a healing, stabilizing field that was later corrupted by negative thoughts and emotions of humanity through millions of years of abuse and torture perpetuated by the controlling dark forces.

MATTER: Vibrating energy.

METAPHYSICAL: Something that is "beyond" the physical, more than the physical, more than the usual.

MIND: The three states of the mind are:

The superconsciousness or the Higher Self: We can reach this level of the mind if we choose to, and then work toward creating and strengthening communication between our conscious self and the Higher Self.

The conscious mind: This is our day-to-day reality. It is like a computer, it becomes and contains whatever data we put into it.

The subconscious mind: This mind is the storehouse. It contains all knowledge and information that we have ever been given. Our Higher Self is the guardian of the subconscious mind, and when we are ready, a portion of information can and will rise to the surface to be redeemed and utilized by the conscious mind.

The superconscious mind has access to the conscious *and* the subconscious mind.

The conscious mind does *not* have full access to the subconscious mind.

The conscious mind *does* have access to the superconscious mind.

The subconscious mind does *not* have access to the conscious *nor* the superconscious mind.

PARANORMAL: Apart from normal. Beyond the range of normal experience or scientific explanation.

PRIME CREATOR: The Ultimate One of all that is— Source Energy. Prime Creator is pure light and love comprised of equal parts of masculine and feminine energy in perfect balance. It is One Great Consciousness.

REPTILIAN: A civilization that originated from the constellation Orion and one is of the early species who occupied our planet.

SOUL: Through the desire of Prime Creator, we were sent forth as individual souls, as spiritual expressions of the One. Prime Creator chose to divide Itself into fragments of consciousness in order to experience more of Itself in all forms and realities, and we are those fragments. We are all spiritual expressions of the One Great Consciousness.

SOUL AGREEMENT or SOUL CONTRACT: Before assuming physical form, a soul will cocreate a life plan that includes karma that the soul wishes to clear, learning that is required if one wants to advance in evolution, service to others in some capacity, or perhaps just for the experience. The plan may consist of many other souls, all in agreement regarding karma, lessons, service to others, or any other situation.

STARSEED: A soul that is seeded from another star system onto a planet, one who has the desire to experience life in all forms and realities. They are explorers, adventurers, and eager to move forward in evolution. Many come in with the express purpose of helping others and assisting in the healing and liberation of the planet and its inhabitants.

UNIVERSE: A universe is a portion of space. There are numerous universes throughout Creation. Our universe is one of a cluster of seven.

$\mathcal{M}y$ Credentials

I am a galactic being having a human experience. I am a Starseed, a Lightworker, a teacher, a healer, a writer, and a spiritual counselor. I am a wife, mother, grandmother, sister, and aunt.

Some years ago, I was searching for a facility where I could host meetings, and when I came upon one that I deemed suitable, I inquired about renting space from them. The owner/manager of the facility then asked what I wanted it for. My answer was, "To teach classes." The next question I was asked was, "Do you have a university degree?"

I do not have a university degree with letters after it.

I do, however, have a *universal* degree with symbols after it. The symbols are hearts. My area of expertise is called "The Knowledge of the Ancients." I have acquired an understanding that every soul has access to;

it is a vast storehouse of knowledge that is accessible via the heart.

My tuition was earned through determination, dedication, and countless hours of doing the necessary inner work. My authority is sourced from a higher vibration.

$\mathcal{A}$cknowledgments

My first and foremost gratitude for all the guidance, support, and love I have received in the writing of this book is to my Higher Self and my beloved Star family. Their words at the onset were:

"You cannot write a wrong book. Just come from the heart."

I have done my best to follow my heart while writing, for that is where my truth resides.

The appreciation, gratefulness, and love that I feel for my husband, Merv, my steadfast friend and companion who has walked by my side for sixty Earth years, is difficult to find the proper words for. He has taken a step back and provided me with unconditional love so that I am able to do the work I am destined to do. He has, in his own way, sacrificed his retirement in order to give me freedom and space without question so that I can bring my work to fruition. He is my rock, my protector, my love, and my support.

Our three sons, their mates, and my extended family have all remained steadfast in their love, acceptance, and loyalty, even though they do not always understand my journey. My heart is full of gratitude for all of them.

My heartfelt thanks goes to all those souls who have sat with me in my groups for the past ten years, for without them, I would have no one to teach. They have taught me as well and enriched my spiritual life in countless ways. To each of them, I say thank you.

Then there are the ones who have been my leaders, teachers, and way-showers, the ones who have taken me through the magical, mystical world of Reiki, tai chi, crystals, shamanism, astrology, numerology, destiny cards, tarot cards, UFOs, and massage therapy, as well as those who have shown me the open door to the world of natural healing and natural medicine. Their numbers are many, and I send them all gratitude.

I feel very blessed to have the opportunity to be here on this planet at this time in Her history and to be able to do the work that I came here to do.

Bethel

Made in the USA
Middletown, DE
10 February 2023